THE COLLECTED POEMS OF SIDNEY KEYES

THE COLLECTED POEMS OF SIDNEY KEYES

Edited
with a Memoir and Notes by
Michael Meyer

ROUTLEDGE
London and New York

First published in 1945 and
reprinted in 1945, 1946, 1951 and 1962
This edition first published in 1988 by Routledge
11 New Fetter Lane, London EC4P 4EE

Published in the USA by Routledge
in association with Methuen Inc.
29 West 35th Street, New York, NY 10001

Set in Linotron Ehrhardt 10 on 12pt
by Input Typesetting Ltd, London SW19 8DR
and printed in Great Britain
by The Guernsey Press Co. Ltd,
Guernsey, Channel Islands

ISBN 0–415–00218–4

CONTENTS

PREFACE TO THE 1988 EDITION

When in 1943 Herbert Read asked me to prepare a volume of Sidney Keyes' collected poems for publication, we agreed that I should do as Edmund Blunden had done with Wilfred Owen and exclude anything that seemed inferior. Keyes himself was, if anything, over-rigorous in this respect; although he chose seventy-two poems for the two volumes he prepared before going to his death in Africa, *The Iron Laurel* and *The Cruel Solstice*. Read and I felt that there were a further twenty-five which we could not ignore, only four of which were written after *The Cruel Solstice* went to press.

Other poems have since come to light. Shortly after the war, a manuscript book was discovered containing over seventy poems which Keyes wrote before leaving Tonbridge School in July 1940. Seven of these (the first seven in the present volume, from *Elegy* to *Greenwich Observatory*) I had known of and published in the 1945 edition. Of the others, only four seemed to me to rise above the average level of adolescent verse, *South Wind, Cathay, Meditation of Phlebas the Phoenician* and *Richmond Park*, and I included these, with a translation of a Catullus poem which I found in one of his letters, in a selection of Keyes' prose which appeared in 1948, *The Minos of Crete*. I have added these five poems here as an appendix, together with eight others not in the 1945 edition or its reprints. Five of these, four 'blues' and a squib which he wrote for my twenty-first birthday, partly to poke fun at my passion for cricket, show Keyes in an unfamiliar light vein; in 1943–4 I excluded them, feeling I suppose that light verse had no place in such a volume. Keyes loved blues, for their words as well as their music, and apart from their intrinsic merit I hope these may help to correct the image of him as an unduly sombre person. Although inclined to be taciturn in a large gathering or among strangers, he was, like Eliot and Orwell, witty and delightful company to his friends. On the few occasions when I met Eliot and the many afternoons and evenings I spent with Orwell, their personalities strongly reminded me of Keyes, not least in their quiet sense of mischief. He had a lot in common with Old Possum.

Of the others, Keyes included *Letter to M.C., 31.vii.41* in *The Iron Laurel*, and I can only think that I omitted it from the original collected poems by an oversight, for which, forty-three years later, I make what must surely be one of the most belated apologies on record.

Keyes' poetry has not diminished with the years. His range was remarkable by any standards: a brilliantly precise observer of landscape and bird life, whether seeing them for themselves (*Pheasant*) or as symbols (*The Kestrels*), he had an unusual gift for entering into and evoking figures from the past who fascinated him (Wordsworth, Clare, Yeats, Schiller, Gilles de Retz, Paul Klee, William Byrd); and in *Lover's Complaint, The Flowering Orchards, The Doubtful Season* and sections two and three of *The Wilderness*, he wrote some of the most individual and moving love poems of this century. Among his poetic masters he numbered Hölderlin and Rilke, and their influence, in particular Rilke's (Keyes' reflections on whom are quoted in my 1944 introduction), adds a dimension to his work which none of his contemporaries or successors has quite equalled, and which can be seen most clearly in such poems as *Four Postures of Death, The Expected Guest* and his two longer works, *The Foreign Gate* and *The Wilderness*. Keyes has sometimes been described as having been obsessed with death, but he was not more so than most of our generation in those years, or our predecessors in 1914–1918.

The fact that Keyes died so young, and in battle, meant that his work was praised for the wrong sentimental reasons, especially and perhaps understandably by older non-combatants, often in terms which Keyes himself, being unsentimental except in love, and inclined to scepticism, would particularly have disliked. Equally understandably, people have tended to dwell overmuch on his lost potential. It is time we stopped mourning what Keyes might have written and assessed him on his achievement.

As recently as 1987 the Headmaster of Dartford Grammar School, Mr. Tony Smith, put me in touch with Mr. James Lucas, the author of several books on military history who, as Private Lucas, had been Keyes' runner in the battle in which he was killed and was one of the last people to see him alive. At my request, Mr. Lucas has written a brief and vivid memoir of Keyes as a soldier, including the first detailed account of his last hours and the manner of his death, and I am grateful to be allowed to print this as an extra appendix.

MICHAEL MEYER
London, 1987

MEMOIR

Sidney Arthur Kilworth Keyes was born at Dartford, Kent, on May 27th, 1922. His mother, the daughter of a Manchester parson, died of peritonitis a few weeks after he was born; his father, Captain Reginald Keyes, had recently returned from war service in India, and the child was entrusted to the care of his paternal grandparents, who also lived at Dartford. Sidney's grandfather, Sidney Kilworth Keyes (whose death he was to commemorate in his first considerable poem, Elegy) dominated his childhood and, indirectly, his whole life. He came of a long line of yeomen farmers, who had lived in Essex for several generations; they had been impoverished by the farming slump of the early 1800's, and he had had to earn his living as a mill-hand. He possessed unusual mental and physical powers and, since he could do anything in the trade from hauling 480 lb. sacks to inventing new gadgets, he quickly rose to the ownership of his own mill: first a windmill, then a water-mill and finally a steam-mill. He became one of the most famous and skilful millers in the country; he patented Daren flour, and was eventually honoured with the freedom of Dartford. The first of his three wives bore the brunt of his early poverty, and died after twelve years of strenuous married life, leaving him with six small children, of whom Reginald, Sidney's father, was the eldest. Reginald was alternately spoilt and severely corrected by his father—his mother was frail, and constantly laid up with childbearing— and grew into an unmanageable child, with such a passion for destruction that his schoolmaster complained of his unscrewing the bolts of his bed as he lay trying to go to sleep. He, too, married three times—Sidney being the child of his second marriage—and died of tuberculosis in 1940.

Sidney lived with his grandparents until he was 9. His father resided there intermittently, but took only a spasmodic interest in him, and a nurse was engaged from the family of one of the mill hands. Sidney was a frail and sickly child, and it was thought unwise to allow him to spend much time out of doors, or to mix with other children. Isolated with his nurse in the great house, except for the relations he saw at meals, he had to create a world of his own to survive. Fortunately he was well equipped, both intellectually and imaginatively, to do so. He quickly learned to read, and gutted books methodically, especially those dealing with legend and history; at the age of 5, *he rejected* The Children's Encyclopaedia *as inaccurate. He also built up a varied menagerie of birds, small animals and reptiles. He did not go to school until he was 9, and his early learning was composed of this curious combination of rustic innocence and antique wisdom. Animals and the heroes of legend and history were more intimate to him than his detached relations. Outwardly he was an amiable child, good-looking, lean and olive-skinned, with fine hazel eyes. Inwardly, he lived among the heroes of his imagination. Almost from the beginning he was split by this duality.*

In 1931, his grandfather, then over 70, married for the third time, and the new Mrs. Keyes immediately sent Sidney to Dartford Grammar School, thus fulfilling his mother's intention. He stayed here for three years, and then took the Common Entrance to Tonbridge, as his father had done.

Keyes found Tonbridge a civilized and tolerant school, and was allowed to pursue his own ways unmolested. He retired into himself, and became an anchorite, though an amiable one; active enough, but with no gift for games. The passions of adolescence left him almost untouched; his chief interests remained books and nature. He had shown at Dartford Grammar School an unusual gift for extempore narration, and he developed into an able history student; although he had started in the bottom form, since at that time he knew no Latin, he reached the Sixth at the age of 16. Here, he was fortunate in his form master. Mr. Tom Staveley was a poet of genuine, though shrouded, talent, whose early work had seriously impressed Yeats, and who was sensitive to any expression of literary promise. He immediately perceived Keyes' gift for narrative and feeling for words, and skilfully directed his reading and criticized his creative work. At 16, Keyes wrote Elegy and Prospero, *the first omens of what was to come.*

In 1939, he visited France; and his whole outlook changed, as though another eye had opened in his head. His vision became, as it were, stereoscopic. He began to see birds and animals as something more than merely beasts of the field; they became significant of deeper values. His writings had hitherto been unusually perceptive adolescent stories and poems. But in July 1940, he wrote The Buzzard. *It marks a turning-point in his literary career; from now on, everything indefinably began to mean something more.*

In October 1940, he went as a history scholar to The Queen's College, Oxford, and at once formed an acquaintance which was largely to determine the future direction of his literary endeavours. John Heath Stubbs shared his tastes and background to an extraordinary degree. He, too, had been forced by an unhappy boyhood to create his own imaginary world—he had been nearly blind from the age of 16—and to speculate on many of the problems that haunted Keyes' mind. For Keyes' memories of his father, and of family life at The Dene, where his tempestuous old grandfather had sometimes thrown the furniture about, were not happy. He had either inherited or been infected with a sense of guilt and of evil destiny. The subject of pain and death fascinated him, and his duality had sharpened since his childhood. That inner chamber of his mind, where he held converse with the heroes of his imagination, had become unapproachable to human beings. It was inhabited only by ghosts and phantoms. Keyes had developed an acute historic sense which enabled him to recreate the very spirits of those who stirred his imagination; and the poet within him dwelt only among the mighty dead. Blake, Schiller, Wordsworth and, above all, Yeats and Rilke, were more intimate to him than the contemporary world. He was in the closest and most constant contact with their minds through their writings, and he preferred their company to that of the living.

Hitherto, Keyes had, perhaps inevitably, found deepest satisfaction in the Romantic poets (1780–1830), with their preoccupation with death and the macabre. Heath Stubbs was able to trace for him the origins of Romanticism in the primitive legends (of which he had a deeper knowledge than Keyes) and its subsequent development through the Mediaeval and, eventually, the Augustan poets. At the same time, he widened Keyes' knowledge of poetic technique, which was not yet adequate for the expression of his varied and complex ideas.*

All this time, the war, even in those dark months, seemed to him remote and unreal. Oxford in wartime is as stifling as a cocoon, and noisy with trivialities. Nor, by the late summer of 1941, had he seriously fallen in love. The contemporary world still seemed to him comparatively unimportant when contrasted with the dark antechamber of his imagination. Later, he was to write the history of his inner mind in the poem Anarchy: *his spiritual autobiography.*

Outwardly, Keyes was still amiable, pensive, impenetrable. His early promise of good looks had not quite been fulfilled; a tendency to anaemia had turned his skin rather sallow, and his face had grown thinner and his nose and cheekbones more prominent. His once fair hair had become dark brown. When he smiled, you noticed the pronounced out-thrust of his upper jaw. He still had magnificent hazel eyes. He had lost something of his

---

* Keyes' literary and artistic preferences are curiously significant. For direction and inspiration, he turned to such visionaries as El Greco, Blake, Hölderlin, Schiller, Rilke, Yeats and Sibelius. At the same time, he found his emotional problems most completely resolved in the writings of the nineteenth-century school of haunted countrymen: Wordsworth, Clare, Van Gogh, Hardy and, later, Housman and Edward Thomas. 'I think I should have been born in the last century in Oxfordshire or Wiltshire, instead of near London between two wars,' he wrote nine weeks before he was killed, 'because then I might have been a good pastoral poet, instead of an uncomfortable metaphysical without roots. The trouble is, that a thing of beauty isn't a joy for ever to me; nor am I content to imagine beauty is truth, etc. All I know is that everything in a vague sort of way means something else, and I want desperately to find out *what*.'

He loved the masters of the macabre: Donne, Webster, Goya, Beddoes, Dickens, Picasso, Klee, Rouault, Graham Greene; and such as came his way of the early German and Russian films.

adolescent aloofness. He mixed well, and this transition became important to him later; it put him in touch with his generation. Yet he never sought the company of any except the very few who he felt had something to give him. He remained fundamentally averse to College activities. He formed his own dramatic society, and produced for them a modern morality play, Hosea, which he had written at Tonbridge. He enjoyed films and pubs. He edited The Cherwell, and got a first in the first half of the war-time history schools.

He was now writing three or four poems a month, in addition to his weekly essay and a number of short stories. By the end of 1941, he had written enough poems to form a volume. He assembled them under the title of The Iron Laurel. They are a study of pain and death from the viewpoint of the necromancer; death is a ghoul, and the poet is a doomed child wandering in a sour land. But after the book had actually been accepted and was about to go to press, Keyes asked the publishers to hold it up until he had completed the long poem which, written at the beginning of 1942, marks the great turning-point in his life. His time at Oxford was nearly at an end, and he realized that in the Army, Death, his pagan god, would be omnipresent. This poem was on a different plane to all that had gone before, a great panorama of the dead in battle: The Foreign Gate. Here, for the first time in his poetry, Death appears as a real presence. The only victory lies in courageous submission. The goal of the soldier is portrayed as an attitude of supreme detachment, of 'active contemplation.' It is the Apollonian conception:

> But help or hope is none till the circle be broken
> Of wishing death and living time's compulsion,
> Of wishing love and living love's destruction.

Keyes entered the Army at Omagh, in Northern Ireland, in April 1942; and for the first time, the poet in him came into immediate contact with the material world. Love and Death, inextricably entwined, became vital problems instead of subjects for laboratory analysis. The world of his imagination blended with the world of reality. He lost his duality. He found his imaginary fears shared by thousands, and became the spokesman of a generation. Inevitably, he abandoned the Apollonian conception, and moved gradually towards the Dionysiac, 'the dolphin's mire and blood.' Death is not a problem that the soldier can solve through 'active contemplation.' A belligerent generation must discover a new solution in the ruck and chaos of battle. Slowly and painfully, Keyes evolved the philosophy of The Wilderness:

> I say, Love is a wilderness and these bones
> Proclaim no failure, but the death of youth.
> We say, You must be ready for the desert

Even among the orchards starred with blossom,
Even in spring, or at the waking moment
When the man turns to the woman, and both are afraid.
All who would save their life must find the desert—
The lover, the poet, the girl who dreams of Christ.
And the swift runner, crowned with another laurel:
They all must face the sun, the red rock desert,
And see the burning of the metal bird.
Until you have crossed the desert and faced that fire
Love is an evil, a shaking of the hand,
A sick pain draining courage from the heart. . . .

And they will find who linger in the garden,
The way of time is not a river but
A pilferer who will not ask their pardon.

Keyes was commissioned in the Queen's Own Royal West Kent Regiment in September 1942, and left England early the following March. He saw only a fortnight's active service. He was killed in action during the last days of the Tunisian campaign on April 29th, 1943.* But on the battlefield he found a serenity which had never been his in England. He had conquered death; the story of his victory is told in his poems.

To understand his war poems, those written between The Foreign Gate and The Wilderness, it is necessary to speak briefly of his conception of the fundamental function of poetry. In an article entitled The Artist in Society, written at about the time of The Foreign Gate, he states this function to be 'to give to his (the poet's) audience some inkling of the continual fusion of finite and infinite, spiritual and physical, which is our world... to express the eternal meaning which resides in the physical world, and show the relationship between the eternal and its physical counterpart.' Nearly a year later, in a letter written to Richard Church in January 1943, he says: 'Rightly or wrongly, I have never tried very assiduously to please Everyman; he is, as you say, a hard master. Nor have I tried to adapt myself to the

---

* As this book was going to press, I received the following account of Keyes' movements after leaving England from Lt.-Col. John M. Haycraft, his C.O. in Tunisia:
'Sidney Keyes came out with the Battalion to Algiers on March 10th, 1943; we moved up by sea to Bone, thence to the Beja sector where we took part in patrol skirmishes only; we then moved to Medjez area and did not, apart from the usual line-holding activity as before, have any serious actions until April 26th, when an attack was made in which Sidney did not take part. On April 29th, however, the battalion attacked a hill, Pt. 133, near Sidi Abdulla, in which Sidney's company took part. His company, C, got its objective successfully during the night. His company commander, Braithwaite, sent Keyes forward with a patrol at dawn to find out the situation as regards the Boche in front. This patrol apparently ran into the enemy, who were forming up for a counter-attack on Hill 133.'
Mr James Lucas, Keyes' runner, who was captured during this action, confirms that Keyes was killed covering his platoon's retreat, and not, as was previously supposed, while a prisoner in enemy hands (see p. 135).

literary fashions of the last few years; I don't even (consciously) follow the present trend towards a new and over-wrought Romanticism. For these reasons, I feel myself rather isolated as a writer; the poets I feel kinship with are dead, yet many people who follow them find me "advanced" and "obscure." The only living writers whom I can accept entirely are Eliot, Charles Williams, Graves (to some extent), my great friend John Heath Stubbs . . . and a few others—very few. As to the question of my symbolism: the best clue that I can give you is to say that I believe the greatest and most influential poets in the last 100 years or so to be Yeats and Rilke. These two brought back reports from a kind of Ultima Thule of Romanticism, which suggest that there is even more—much more—to be discovered there: and the starting point of my quest is therefore an attempt to synthesize this information. When I have fused and assimilated (if ever) this information, I shall be ready to set out. The Second Coming *and* Foreign Gate *are my nearest misses so far; in the meantime, I go on writing and use—perhaps rather wildly—the pastoral and symbolic images that move me most. My only non-poetic influence is, as naturally follows, the psychology of C. G. Jung.'*

This attitude is clarified by an entry in his diary, made at about the same time: 'How significant it is that Hood's ghost in The Haunted House *is a daylight one! The Romantics raised a spectre they could not lay; it was, broadly speaking, death as a part of life, conceived in terms of sensual imagery. To the Middle Ages and the Elizabethans, death was merely the Leveller; to the 17th century, a metaphysical problem; to the 18th century, the end of life. The Romantics tried to think of it as a state of existence. By the 1840's, this had become an obsession, and had degenerated into curiosity. By the later 19th century, and up to our own time, it had resulted in a clearly apparent* Death Wish, *as the only solution to the problem—since the solution must come in sensual terms. It was left to necrophilous Germany, to Rilke in fact, to provide the best solution short of actually dying. That is why there had to be a "Poet of Death" in the 20th century; and why Rilke is the most important poet since Goethe and Wordsworth.'*

In a letter to John Heath Stubbs, dated February 20th, 1943—one of the last he wrote in England—Keyes speaks of Rilke's conception of death as a creature that we bear within us, like a child waiting for birth, and of the necessity for making our own terms with it in its time of triumph. The story of his conquest of death is the story of a voluntary submission; of that abnegation of self which enabled a generation to come straight from the lecture-room and the factory bench to face the ordeal of battle with hope and courage. Every generation must conquer death anew. Richard Hillary has spoken eloquently for the men of action, the natural fighters. Keyes is rather the spokesman of the conscript, the uncourageous anchorite, the separated lover. Their conquest of death was not the fierce embrace of the airman but, in his own words, 'a restless candle-flame, rising clearest at the moment of extinction.'

Keyes must not be thought of as a degenerate Romantic who wooed death. He recognized the danger of the Death Wish, as manifested in the contemporary attitude of the German nation. In the same letter as that in which he speaks of Rilke's conception of death, he writes: 'Your feelings about German art, and the love of death, are only too unfortunately my own. I think any German reader will agree that there is a persistent death wish in German poetry; it finds its highest form in Rilke's conception. . . . But the theme is constant (the whining and whimpering of Mozart's Clarinet Quintet is almost the shudder of a girl touched by her lover), and appears in painting (Matthaeus Grünewald) as well; it is quite as unmistakeable (sic) in the religious yearning of Novalis (19th cen.) as in the "rawhead" graveyard elegies of Gryphius (16th cen.). How can we account for the fact that a whole nation has now gone stark mad with love of death? Because the contemporary German attitude to death appears to be one of hopeless infatuation (mixed with fear and repulsion, but all physical infatuation must be); the whole nation has gone crazy with this passion, always present but now become overriding. . . . Perhaps the Germans are, in a sense, a chosen people; their task is to explore death, just as it has been that of the Jews to explore pain, and of the French (perhaps) to explore the possibilities of pleasure, whether of the intellect or the senses; and to make an art of death, as the Jews have of martyrdom and the French of pleasure. It remains for someone to make an art of love, a much harder task. . . .' But while prepared to submit to the inevitable, he had no intention of becoming a voluntary victim. He continues: 'Please send me your death wish poem quickly, before the general European death wish claims me (though under protest, and with the strongest desire for life, even to old age). . . .' And in his last letter of all, written to Renée-Jane Scott on the afternoon before he was killed, he writes: 'I shall have a lot more to say about this when the time for speaking returns. I cannot think that this campaign can last much longer; but after that, who knows! The only way back seems to be through armed Europe. I am not in much of a hurry, but I will get back sometime if it's humanly possible; and I've never yet failed to do anything I set myself to do. . . .'

He was not 21 when he died. But he must not be thought of as an adolescent prodigy. What he achieved is remarkable, not because of his youth, but for its intrinsic worth. In articulating the dumb courage of a generation, he breathed new life into many of the traditions of English poetry: the dramatic monologue, the landscape, the macabre and, especially, blank verse. Above all, he was the first truly English poet effectively to marry Continental symbolism to the English Romantic tradition; and, with his exceptional sensibility to the face of Nature, his detailed knowledge of legend, and his intuitive assessment of the conjuring power of words, he fashioned symbolism *into a precision instrument. He dreaded obscurity. 'I am not a man but a voice,' he wrote in May* 1942. *'My only justification is my power of speaking clearly.' He realized that implication rather than statement is an essential tenet of symbolism; but he intended to be intelligible to anyone with a reasonable knowledge of history, who had also read the Bible and* The Golden Bough. *The latter he seemed to regard as an indispensable primer of symbolism.*

He was ready to set out. I cannot believe that his creative purpose had been satisfied by these preliminary experiments; his inspiration consisted, not of a series of lyrical impulses, but of a constant and urgent force. The fulfilment of his promise rests with the survivors of his generation.

MICHAEL MEYER.

R.A.F. Station,
High Wycombe, Bucks.
October 1944.

NOTE TO THE 1945 EDITION

Some of these poems originally appeared in *The Fortnightly*, *The Listener*, *English*, *The New Statesman and Nation*, *Modern Reading*, *Horizon*, *Kingdom Come*, *Poetry* (London), *The Cherwell*, *The St. Martin's Review*, *Bugle Blast* (Messrs. Ivor Nicholson and Watson), *Poetry Quarterly*, *Poetry Folios*, *More Poems from the Forces* (Messrs. Routledge), *Poetry in Wartime* (Messrs. Faber and Faber), and *Oxford Poetry*, 1943 (Basil Blackwell); others in *The Iron Laurel* (July 1942) and *The Cruel Solstice* (January 1944), both published by Messrs. Routledge. Messrs. Hurst and Blackett have kindly allowed extracts to be reprinted from an article *The Artist in Society*, which Keyes contributed to a collection of essays entitled *The Future of Faith*; and Messrs. Heinemann have permitted me to use in the Memoir some of the matter contained in a briefer tribute which appeared in the first number of *The Windmill*.

But especially I must thank those relatives and friends of Keyes without whose patient and generous assistance this book could never have been compiled: his stepmother, Mrs. Violet Keyes, Miss Phyllis Keyes, Dr. Muriel Keyes, Mrs. Renée-Jane Johnson, Miss Milein Cosmann, Mr. Tom Staveley, Mr. Basil Taylor, Mr. Percy B. Meyer, Mr. and Mrs. E. J. H. Eames, Mr. Richard Church, Mr. Herbert Read, and Mr. John Heath Stubbs. The last-named was in the closest and most constant touch with Keyes during the whole of the latter's most fruitful literary period and often discussed poems with him while they were still in progress. Many of the notes are the product of his accurate memory.

The poems have been arranged as far as possible in chronological order, except that *The Wilderness* has been placed in what seems its rightful position at the climax of the book, i.e. after the two or three comparatively slight poems which followed it. Some thirty poems of obviously inferior merit have been omitted, although a few such (e.g. *Not Chosen*) have been included for their documentary interest. No trace has been found of the poems which Keyes is known to have written in Africa, and they must be assumed to have perished with him.

M.M.

Elegy

(*In memoriam S. K. K.*)

APRIL again, and it is a year again
Since you walked out and slammed the door
Leaving us tangled in your words. Your brain
Lives in the bank-book, and your eyes look up
Laughing from the carpet on the floor:
And we still drink from your silver cup.

It is a year again since they poured
The dumb ground into your mouth:
And yet we know, by some recurring word
Or look caught unawares, that you still drive
Our thoughts like the smart cobs of your youth—
When you and the world were alive.

A year again, and we have fallen on bad times
Since they gave you to the worms.
I am ashamed to take delight in these rhymes
Without grief; but you need no tears.
We shall never forget nor escape you, nor make terms
With your enemies, the swift departing years.

July 1938.

Prospero

THIS is no man: a disembodied mind,
Spinning in its own orbit like the earth;
A voice grown old with words and dreamy-rapt
In its own cadences—as one might say,
A little tired of always speaking truth.
He knows all secrets of the earth and air
And of men's hearts. There is no more surprise
For him in anything, nor can he hate
For long, e'en those who overthrew his rule
Temporal—for so powerful is his heart
That worldly things before it pale. Who cares
What fate may come to kings or dukes, when graves
Ope at his words and ghosts do pay him homage?
When spirits hasten on the eager winds
To do his bidding, and the elements
Wait his command? Oh, he might be a God
If he but chose; his voice peals out
In the dread thunder; his all-powerful sword
The keen blue lightning; his eye the moon;
The winds his messengers, the very sea
His counsellor, which mutters all day long
Words of great meaning, understood by none
But Prospero. He should be a God!
Yet he is not. He loves, and through his soul
Spreads a great tenderness for all alive:
For men and beasts; for gentle Ariel;
For clouds and flowers, all beauty of the earth.
He pities the cold moon, because she weeps
All night, upon a world which has no need
Of tears, for it is beautiful. Its griefs,
Cloud-shadows fleeing swiftly o'er a wood
In springtime. He is far too wise to weep
For fallen blossoms, or for youth that's gone.
He knows the spring must always come again
E'en though the sap is withered for a space
Within the bole; and that the stream flows on
Beneath its icy mantle. So, he smiles,
For all that's past must soon return again—
That is the law. Life's but a summer gnat

2

Whiling away its plaintive hour in play,
But immortality's a frozen flower.
He walks the soaring night among the stars,
Which throng about him, children who would hear
Some trifling tale, of how on earth true love
Came to fruition; how an old man died
And yet was born again, for sweeter sleep.
Such tales he loves to tell. Though his clear eye
Could outstare Death, and make him powerless,
'Tis not his will to do so. Death, to him
No spectre, is a fellow-sorcerer,
His only rival. Why should Prosper fear
A colleague in his Art? When those two meet,
They will yarn on for hours of charms and spells,
Discuss the properties of mandrake-root,
And argue whether wolf's-bane or hemlock
Is better sleeping potion. Death, at last,
Drowsy, a little bored with Prosper's talk,
Will doze away, wrapt in that droning voice.
So they will watch, those two, till all the stars
Fall from the sky; till even time is done,
And on them creeps eternity, a sea
Of quietness, while they dream on in peace.

1938.

Nocturne for four voices

One.   NIGHT again, look at the sky:
              Slow cold clouds strangle the sun.
              Night's a black panther walking in the trees.
              Look at the sky and weep, for all your fun
              Is over, no more laughter: do not dare
              To laugh, or hands will seize you by the hair
              And drag you high, high, high,
              Through shrill ways of the upper air.
              There is a frightened whisper in the leaves.

Two.   My true love's gone and I'm alone—
              The night, the night is all my joy.
              My heart's as heavy as a stone—
              Come night, come sleep, my only joy.
              I cannot sleep since he is gone:
              It's hard to learn to sleep alone.
              Come night, sleep, death, my only joy.

Three.   If there should never be another dawn,
              And this were your last night? You fool,
              How do you know you're safe?
              Fool, fool.

One.   Look at the sky.

Three.   If all the world were turned away.
              What could you do, you fool?
              Why should there ever be a dawn?

Two.   My life, my love, he looked on me;
              His lips were red as the hawberry.
              His eyes they shone like dew on a rose:
              Where the dead go to, nobody knows.

All Three.   Where the dead go to, nobody knows.

Four.   This is the time

4

When it is best to be afraid,
To turn away
From song and sigh
And take your rest
In night's dark breast
And under his drooping eyelids' shade.

Three.   Do not sleep, do not sleep. Watch the hours
Flit like moths among the flowers;
The moon's a clock without any hands,
The brook is running hourglass sands.
Do not sleep—you are a pawn
In time's mad game. Wait for the dawn.
Do not sleep.

One.   The sky flows deep
As spring tide in the Atlantic, and the stars
Are drowned men's eyes, tangled in floating spars
Of trees. The moon's a swollen corpse.
Look at the sky and drown yourself.

Three.   If you dare!

One.   Drown yourself.

Three.   You could not bear
Another dawn
Or the anarchic starlings on the lawn.
Sleep indeed, sleep in the earth
And spare your soul another birth.

One.   Drown yourself.

Four.   Sleep is sweet in the tomb
As in your quiet room.
Do not fear, every bed is a bier
Sleep is sweet in the grave and the womb.

One.   Drown yourself.

Four.   Sleep is sweet in the womb and the grave.

One.   Drown yourself.

Four.	Why trouble to save This wisp of vapour called a soul From creeping out of its tiny hole Like a mouse From his cramped house?
Two.	They took my love away All smiling dead. They laid him in the clay— Our marriage bed.
One.	Swirl, rolled in under-pulling currents Through the sky: choke and drown Deep down Among the seaweeds and the corals red: Among the swimming planets in the deep Sea-swell of sleep: Among the teeming constellations Smiling dead.
Three.	You will not see the sun again Nor hear the hurrying footsteps of the rain.
Four.	The fury in your head Will cease, and all your sickly wondering, When you are dead.
One.	Then drown yourself.
Two.	My love's asleep all in the ground, The grass grows green on his grave-mound. He's lain there a year or more, Yet still I weep as I did before. His eyes were stars, his lips were coral-red: On his death-day we were wed. Death took my own, my sweetest boy— So come, sweet death, and be my joy.
All Four.	So come, sweet night So come, sweet sleep So come, sweet death And be my joy.

July 1939.

6

Lament for dead symbolists

DOWN those long balconies of evening
Resounds the progress of an April ghost:
Let living listen while the dying sing
Nor seek to interpret what our spring has lost.

The childish promises of lilac
Seduce the corpse and break his serenade;
Willows and Wagner sigh like
The sentimental gossip of a shade.

Taking this old frayed hand to kiss
Its wisdom in the posy of a ring
Memory sickens. So it's come to this—
Beauty a half-truth, love is everything.

That was the fallacy of their dream,
The reason for their haunting and our quest.
The quiet insistence of the falling stream
And beauty's worship wearies the oppressed.

These balconies are empty, though the scent
Of tender indecision wanders there;
Let night proclaim their punishment
Erasing gallant fictions from the air.

Their balustrades beckoning no true lover
Wake only to salute a falling star:
Only night's plectrum once again strums over
The fingering of their cracked guitar.

Nefertiti

QUEEN Nefertiti, O she was a high proud queen;
Her fingers were obelisks
And the red copper discs
Of virginity hung from her ears.
Nobody knows what she has seen
Walking in the desert with fates and fears.

Queen Nefertiti was gently curved
As a dancing snake or an antelope's horn.
Nobody knows what monsters she has borne;
And foreign kings, we understand,
Were filled with shame and all unnerved
To see her dancing on the sand.

Queen Nefertiti, gentle as a cow,
Worshipped the moon's white horns
Whose masculinity adorns
The placid meadow of her brow.
And disappointed suitors whisper that
She was love-stricken for a tabby-cat.

Queen Nefertiti, O she had no lover:
Sometimes she kissed a flower,
Or in her bitter hour
She sang to the stars complainingly;
And knowing that the golden age was over
She longed to sleep with stones or stroke the sea.

Fragment: 'Shall the dead return?'

FROGS croak. The secret water,
Muscular, fumbles blunt boulders.
No other sound. This glassy peace is spring.
Nothing remains, except remembering
Lost childish ecstasies of evening;
Under my body lying here
The earth beats like a dynamo, pumping sap,
Pumping the blood through all life's arteries.
If the dead indeed awake and return,
Then it's these spring nights they choose.
Pain for them is this awakening;
They stray wearily, grey faces wistful,
Seeking and yearning for eternity.
But no Nirvana for them. Even the grave
Feels the spring rain, and the rotten dead lover
Awakes a moment to grope and know
He is alone:
Oh, sour and cold echoes the cuckoo's cry
Through the bare galleries of the skull.
Yes, they are whispering among the poplars,
They stand in the further furrows like scarecrows
Scraggy and silent and watching immobile.
In spring they all come back:
I saw old Housman waiting by the weir
For sweethearts he never knew and never will know,
They all come back.
But surely for me this beauty is enough
Always like this to live, and never die,
Watching while iridescent duck-wings carve
In wild geometry the evening sky. . . .

Greenwich Observatory

THIS onion-dome holds all intricacies
Of intellect and star-struck wisdom; so
Like Coleridge's head with multitudinous
Passages riddled, full of strange instruments
Unbalanced by a touch, this organism
From wires and dials spins introverted life.
It never looks, squat on its concrete shoulders,
Down at the river's swarming life, nor sees
Crane's groping insect-like activity
Nor slow procession of funnels past the docks.
Turning its inner wheels, absorbed in problems
Of space and time, it never hears
Birds singing in the park or children's laughter.
Alive, but in another way, it broods
On this its Highgate, hypnotized
In lunar reverie and calculation.
Yet night awakes it; blind lids open
Leaden to look upon the moon:
A single goggling telescopic eye
Enfolds the spheric wonder of the sky.

April 1940.

The buzzard

THIS town curled round a hilltop
Flattened and steeply canted at the sun
Sleeps like a brown snake. The poplars point
Tapering shadows, pendula of fate
Across the turf. The golden sun revolves
On the invisible radius of time
And tufts of cloud swim round, dissolving
Or reappearing as the currents of the moment
Vary up there.
               Life swings on its axis
In motion centripetal to this sphere
Or dust under the burning-glass of sky:
This noontide motion spins a kind of peace.
Thoughts nuzzle too the crystalline
Walls of the curving brain and gape their message
Dumbly and flounce away. A caterpillar
Measures with looping back a mulberry leaf;
This is another way of portioning
The endless moment, another demonstration
Of time's deceit and the geometry of living.
A point projected from the hill's brown arc
Draws out its tangent from the central
And unexpected angle of a tower;
Then comes to rest in space at last, suspended
From the sun's further circle as a spider
Hangs from a twig from unseen filaments.

The buzzard's unreflective eye
Quick swivelling on its axis, concentrates
All planes and angles into one great sphere
Of earth its prey. The terra-cotta town
Dropped on the hill, generates circles spreading
To the horizon; rings of green and grey
Granite or yellow of mimosa thickets
Spin round the central pivot of his vision.
Only the quiet eye of water
Stares back and challenges the symmetry.
Behind the buzzard's lens, all secrets
Of beauty or of form unapprehended,
Life's many meanings blend their rays to one

11

Bright spot of cruelty within his brain.
Buzzard drops down the sky and shadows straddle
Longer on grass and rock. Now dust clouds rise
Along the tracks; a herd of goats stray past;
Their noise shatters the meaning of the moment
And breaks the circle of extended peace.
Why should we wish to hide within the present,
Hanging above infinity and waiting
For pain to move, a rabbit in the grass?
Unfocus rather the too-watchful eye
And wander singing in the golden haze
Behind the flock, and take with them your pleasure
At random from each leaf or twig. So break
The trance of living symmetry, disprove
The buzzard's callous theorem of small pain
And sprawl at last under a myrtle-tree,
Breathing the fleshy odour of its leaves.
So find a better variant of peace,
Another meaning and another science
In nightfall's final clemency of quiet.

July 1940.

Cervières

LOOK, Aimée, and you, Victor, look—
The birds have taken all our cherries—
Down in the brown-walled orchard on the hillside
The cherry-trees are weeping for their fruit;
Only the clusters of green stalks
Remain; the stones are scattered on the grass.
There will be no more cherries, not this summer
Nor next, if we get another. God!
It's beyond bearing that they eat our cherries
And fly away and leave the trees in mourning.
Soon an invader will be taking more than cherries:
They'll be stealing our dreams or breaking up
Our history for firewood.

12

Children, see
The avenues of cherry-trees are broken
And trampled boughs crawl in the dust. See, Victor,
How the sun bouncing off the mountain strikes
Christ's wooden throat above the cemetery:
Flesh broken like our cherry-trees and ravished.
The path runs open and smiling down the hill;
It leaps the walls and hides behind the ruins.

Now take this moment and create its image
Impregnable to time or trespasser,
And turn your mind to realize your loss.
The cherry-trees are broken and their fruit
Sown on the indecipherable mountains.
Realize your loss and take it in your hands
And turn it like a pebble. You perceive
It has a stone's dumb smell; its patterns
Plot some forgotten map. Regard your loss.

Planting this lump of pain, perhaps a flower
Might burst from it; perhaps a cherry-tree,
Perhaps a world or a new race of men.

Regard your loss. The blossoms of the cherry
Are rotten now; the branch is violated;
The fruit is stolen and our dreams have failed.
Yet somewhere—O beyond what bitter ranges?—
A seed drops from the sky and like a bomb
Explodes into our orchard's progeny,
And so our care may colonize a desert.
They cannot break our trees or waste our dreams,
For their despoiling is a kind of sowing.

Aimée and Victor, stop crying. Can't you understand
They cannot steal our cherries or our joy?
Let them take what they want, even our dreams.
Somewhere our loss will plant a better orchard.

September 1940.

Remember your lovers

YOUNG men walking the open streets
Of death's republic, remember your lovers.

When you foresaw with vision prescient
The planet pain rising across your sky
We fused your sight in our soft burning beauty:
We laid you down in meadows drunk with cowslips
And led you in the ways of our bright city.
Young men who wander death's vague meadows,
Remember your lovers who gave you more than flowers.

When truth came prying like a surgeon's knife
Among the delicate movements of your brain
We called your spirit from its narrow den
And kissed your courage back to meet the blade—
Our anaesthetic beauty saved you then.
Young men whose sickness death has cured at last,
Remember your lovers and covet their disease.

When you woke grave-chilled at midnight
To pace the pavement of your bitter dream
We brought you back to bed and brought you home
From the dark antechamber of desire
Into our lust as warm as candle-flame.
Young men who lie in the carven beds of death,
Remember your lovers who gave you more than dreams.

From the sun sheltering your careless head
Or from the painted devil your quick eye,
We led you out of terror tenderly
And fooled you into peace with our soft words
And gave you all we had and let you die.
Young men drunk with death's unquenchable wisdom,
Remember your lovers who gave you more than love.

October 1940

Sour land

AT Stanton Harcourt in Oxfordshire there is an ancient tower in
which Pope completed the fifth book of his *Iliad*, when illness and
disillusionment were beginning to oppress him.

I

The houses are white stone in this country,
Windowless and blind as leprosy;
No peace for the wanderer waiting only death.
Plovers crouch in the rain between the furrows
Or wheel club-winged and tumble across the wind;
A land so dead ghosts lodge not
Along its borders to torment the mind.
No ghosts, but another terror; every naked road
Of this sour land harbours a running demon
Who jogs along the fallow all night long
Black under moonlit cloud though shadowless;
Even by day the acrid-tasting air
Reveals his presence to the introspective.
The ponds are cloudy, filled with eyeshot corpses
Of servant girls who drowned themselves for spite.
This landscape of bulbous elm and stubble
Sharpens the mind into revolt at last.

II

So to his perch appropriate with owls
The old lame poet would repair,
When sorrow like a tapeworm in his bowels
Drove him to Troy and other men's despair.

His lame leg twisted on the spiral stair,
He cursed the harsher canker in his heart;
Then in the turret he would scrawl and glare
And long to pull his enemies apart.

When night came knocking at the panes
And bats' thin screeching pierced his head,
He thought of copulation in the lanes
And bit his nails and praised the glorious dead.

15

At dawn the lapwings cried and he awoke
From dreams of Paris drowned in Helen's hair;
He drew his pride about him like a cloak
To face again the agony of the stair.

III

O friend, if you should venture to that country,
Pass guardedly, be unseduced
By its too subtle promises of peace;
Its quiet is of a kind you should not seek.
Look not about you overmuch
Nor listen by the churchyard wall
Lest you should hear the words as soft as nightfall
Of death in promises kind but lecherous indeed.
Heed not the spirit of the twisted ash
Who counsels how to tie the noose;
Neither the spirit calling under the bridge
Where the long eel-grass twists to strangulation.
The sullen girl who smiles and shows her teeth
Is rather more than the common type of slut:
The old man ploughing against the wind
Turns over more than soil; or in the pasture
Two men are digging not a trench—
A grave for all you know and all you hope.
Remember the weasel questing down the hedge,
The dead crow hanging from the oak.
This is a very ancient land indeed;
Aiaia formerly or Cythera
Or Celidon the hollow forest called;
This is the country Ulysses and Hermod
Entered afraid; by ageing poets sought
Where lives no love nor any kind of flower—
Only the running demon, thought.

November 1940.

William Yeats in Limbo

WHERE folds the central lotus
Flesh and soul could never seek?
Under what black-scar'd mountain
May Pallas with Adonis meet?

Spirit-bodies' loveliness
Cannot expiate my pain:
How should I learn wisdom
Being old and profane?

My thoughts have swarmed like bees
In an old ruined tower:
How should I go to drive them out
Lacking joy and power?

How could I learn youth again,
With figured symbols weaving
Truth so easily, now I
Am old and unbelieving?

By what chicanery of time
May sword and sheath be separated?
Silent be the singer who thinks of me
And how I was defeated.

December 1940.

Being not proud

BEING not proud to praise a lonely man's
Heroic loveless dream-humility most often
Comes to the drunken or the moonstruck mind—
I seek new pain to soften
Like rain the stony soil, or careful wind.

Moses' great parleying on Sinai
Brought anger on him and defeat:
Love, being no frigid stonecrop flower,
Blooms not among pride's wrack and sleet
Nor ornaments an introverted tower.

The bones of heroes crowned with stone and statue
Nourish no flower nor bitter cry;
Yet groping painfully, love's roots may save
The dumb soul of a stone, or justify
The holed heart in a crossroad grave.

December 1940.

Advice for a journey

THE drums mutter for war and soon we must begin
To seek the country where they say that joy
Springs flowerlike among the rocks, to win
The fabulous golden mountain of our peace.

O my friends, we are too young
For explorers, have no skill nor compass,
Nor even that iron certitude which swung
Our fathers at their self-fulfilling North.

So take no rations, remember not your homes—
Only the blind and stubborn hope to track
This wilderness. The thoughtful leave their bones
In windy foodless meadows of despair.

Never look back, nor too far forward search
For the white Everest of your desire;
The screes roll underfoot and you will never reach
Those brittle peaks which only clouds may walk.

Others have come before you. The immortal
Live like reflections and their frozen faces
Will give you courage to ignore the subtle
Sneer of the gentian and the iceworn pebble.

The fifes cry death and the sharp winds call.
Set your face to the rock; go on, go out
Into the bad lands of battle, into the cloud-wall
Of the future, my friends, and leave your fear.

Go forth, my friends, the raven is no sibyl;
Break the clouds' anger with your unchanged faces.
You'll find, maybe, the dream under the hill—
But never Canaan, nor any golden mountain.

5th March 1941.

Two variations

I

THE warm night curves around me like a hand;
Thus after the intricacies of day
The open windows and the stone-eyed bishop
Books' eager faces and the necessity for love
It brings me certainty in every breath.

Beyond what vision watches God's white face?
What tombstone thought may hide His beating heart?
And have I heard Him speak yet? In the night
Truth comes much easier, no more afraid
Of the clock's questioning and the plaster skull.

There is no revelation, says the darkness;
Only lie down in hope like children
Waking to empty Sunday morning
And the silly voices of pigeons in the tower.

II

It is not you I believe in but your silence.
When rainclouds leaned across this smooth-tongued city
And even the staircase smelt of summer
I followed you that day but never found you.

When shadows hung about the streets
And every pinnacle stood sharp at dusk
I looked for you that time but never saw you.
It is not you I worship but your wisdom.

Graven in moonlight every thought and moment
Serene the folded eyes of pediments
Your face was empty and acanthus-crowned.
It is not you I fear but your great glory.

March 1941.

Elegy for Mrs. Virginia Woolf

UNFORTUNATE lady, where white crowfoot binds
Unheeded garlands, starred with crumpled flowers,
Lie low, sleep well, safe from the rabid winds
Of war and argument, our hierarchies and powers.

Let the clear current spare you, once
A water spirit, spare your quiet eyes;
Let worm and newt respect your diffidence—
And sink, tired lovely skull, beyond surprise.

Over that head, those small distinguished bones
Hurry, young river, guard their privacy;
Too common, by her grave the willow leans
And trails its foliage fittingly.

In time's retreat, a stickleback's
Most complicated house, she lies:
Colours and currents tend her; no more vex
Her river-mind our towns and broken skies.

Paul Klee

THE short-faced goblins with their heavy feet
Trampled your dreams, their spatulate
Fingers have torn the tracery of your wisdom:
But childlike you would not cry out, transforming
Your enemies to little angry phantoms
In clarity of vision exorcized.
Until at last they conquered by attrition,
And draining the last dregs of love away,
They left you from the angular
Prison of primary fears no way but flight:
Yet never could invade your waterworld of spirit
Since half divining there among the dance
Of shadowed currents lurking ever
Their unguessed image, luminous with fear.
And so they stirred the shallows till the sky
Flew blue in shards and thought sank even deeper,
Where crouched your passion's residue confined:
The evil centre of a child's clear mind.

5th April 1941.

Poem for May the first

IN May brought down and blinkered
When summer calls the tune and fondles
Fond wish not will, as the magnolia's candles
Burn white to greet the courteous evening light,
I have my strength, yet lack ability.

Having desire, yet without energy
My fingers trace the soft-faced season's features
Too easily, forgetting all the strictures
They learnt in picking sharper strings and hardly
Stray to May's chord, nor seek the blackthorn's secret.

Others have made the May since Juliet
Held in her face four centuries of summer,
Creating a pedantic myth. We later
Must root in print our young endeavour
Without the promise of an August saviour.

Having no increase but the willing labour
As tulips gulp the sun, of procreation,
I praise this unheroic generation
Anchored to earth and confident and hopeless
Of bloom this May as any wry-limbed cypress.

5th May 1941.

Poem for Milein Cosmann

SUMMER. The fine rain speckles
My windowsill, and beyond heavy trees
A blackbird sings, green voice of May.
And I the summer's prisoner,
Remembering earlier promise, the safety
Of flowering trees with the unlucky hawthorn
Still beautiful not deadly, thank you
For all your kindness, for restoring
These gardens and my singing voice in May.

May 1941.

23

Gilles de Retz

MARSHAL of France. The prancing horses
And banners licking the air. I tell you now,
Standing in pride who have no bright cuirass,
That was not half the glory, not a jot of it.
Now, velvet-draped like a coffin with nothing inside
But the echo of nails, remembering the hammer's
Talk in an empty vault, all I can do is tell you
God's mercy to me when I was alive.
I have seen angels marching—others also
Armed but all strong as morning, among the trumpets;
Though I am young, God's anger like a woman
Fought by my side three years, then was extinguished
In flame, the old sign, the old blazon shining.
It comes strange ways, the pure divine anger,
Piercing your safety like a lancet, or perhaps
A flat knife working for years behind the eyes,
Distorting vision. That is the worst of all.
Or a boy's voice flowering out of silence
Rising through choirs to the ear's whorled shrine
And living there, a light.

                         What if I sought that glory
When, sign forgotten, fire had darkened my image
Of pure bright anger? What if indeed I danced
Another figure, seeking pain's intricate
Movements to weave that holy exultation?
Knife in the head before, now in the hand
Makes little difference. Pain is never personal;
As love or anger unconfined, it takes
Part in each moment and person, unconditioned
By time or identity, like an atmosphere.
There is no giving or receiving, only
Pain and creation coming out of pain.
Now I have made you angry; but think of this—
Which is the stronger, my pain or your love?
Old men like towers separate in the evening.

Six score in a year, I tell you. The high white bed,
Caesar's pleasures, and the dry well. See
How I believed in pain, how near I got
To living pain, regaining my lost image

Of hard perfection, sexless and immortal.
Nearer than you to living love, to knowing
The community of love without giving or taking
Or ceasing or the need of change. At least
I knew this in my commonwealth of pain.
You, knowing neither, burn me and fear my agony
And never learn any better kind of love.
Six score, then raising Lucifer by guile,
I sinned. It was unnecessary; so
It is for you to punish me. But remember
Never a man of you fought as I those years
Beside the incarnation of mortal pride,
The yearning of immortals for the flesh.
Nor will you ever feel God's finger
Probing your soul's anatomy, as I
Have been dissected these five years; for never
Since Christ has any man made pain so glorious
As I, nor dared to seek salvation
Through love with such long diligence as I through pain.

Have mercy, Lord, on misdirected worship.
On this soul dressed for death in hot black velvet.
Bishop of Nantes, cover the Cross.

16th May 1941.

Europe's prisoners

NEVER a day, never a day passes
But I remember them, their stoneblind faces
Beaten by arclights, their eyes turned inward
Seeking an answer and their passage homeward:

For being citizens of time, they never
Would learn the body's nationality.
Tortured for years now, they refuse to sever
Spirit from flesh or accept our callow century.

Not without hope, but lacking present solace,
The preacher knows the feel of nails and grace;
The singer snores; the orator's facile hands
Are fixed in a gesture no one understands.

Others escaped, yet paid for their betrayal:
Even the politicians with their stale
Visions and cheap flirtation with the past
Will not die any easier at the last.

The ones who took to garrets and consumption
In foreign cities, found a deeper dungeon
Than any Dachau. Free but still confined
The human lack of pity split their mind.

Whatever days, whatever seasons pass,
The prisoners must stare in pain's white face:
Until at last the courage they have learned
Shall burst the walls and overturn the world.

21st May 1941.

The anti-symbolist

IF one could only be certain beyond all question
That nature evolved through a zodiac of symbols
Upon an axis of creative mind:
Then one might plan in expectation
Of enlightenment, a perfect revolution
Or at least repetition, and escape suspense.
But nothing seems related, incident or vision,
To any but an arbitrary thought:
The wind moving between the cypresses
Stirs only single leaf, stale wreath. To them
Fighting the roots and drowned beyond memory
Under the cypresses, there is no word for Wind,
And the wind never dies. The tall old woman
Eating her sandwiches on a pompous vault
And her dog who loves to play tag with tombstones,
Need never recur, yet link me with the drowned ones
Of earth, quite unforgettably.

We should not work that way. Anticipation
Is crooked thinking, for nature unobserved
Revolving never, remains its own reflection.
And time flows through us from its sources
Toward the unguessed waterfall, the desert
Of dry eternity; as old men in Greece
Saw dimly its current and our black Niagara.
Forward is not our business; but the higher
Reaches may at least be mapped
With some small boast of skill and application—
And enough science to arrive at morning
Without undue surprise or any fear
Before the estuary lashed with pain, the sharp
Lift of the bar, and feel the tide making westward.
Then only in that drowned man's paradise
Of Hy Brasil or currentless Sargasso,
May the dead and the wind and the old woman
And her dog and my over-curious mind
Meet neighbourly and mingle without question.

23rd May 1941.

Plowman

TIME was I was a plowman driving
Hard furrows, never resting, under the moon
Or in the frostbound bright-eyed morning
Labouring still; my team sleek-hided
As mulberry leaves, my team my best delight
After the sidelong blade my hero.
My iron-shod horses, my heroic walkers.
Now all that's finished. Rain's fallen now
Smudging my furrows, the comfortable
Elms are windpicked and harbour now no singer
Or southward homing bird; my horses grazing
Impossible mountain-sides, long-frogged and lonely.
And I'm gone on the roads, a peevish man
Contending with the landscape, arguing
With shrike and shrewmouse and my face in puddles;
A tiresome man not listened to nor housed
By the wise housewife, not kissed nor handled
By any but wild weeds and summer winds.
Time was I was a fine strong fellow
Followed by girls. Now I keep company
Only with seasons and the cold crazy moon.

June 1941.

St. John Baptist

I, John, not reed but root;
Not vested priest nor saviour but a voice
Crying daylong like a cricket in the heat,
Demand your worship. Not of me
But of the traveller I am calling
From beyond Jordan and the limestone hills,
Whose runner and rude servant I am only.
Not man entirely but God's watchman,
I dwell among these blistered rocks
Awaiting the wide dawn, the wonder
Of His first coming and the Dove's descent.

June 1941.

28

A garland for John Clare

I

WHETHER the cold eye and the failing hand
Of these defrauded years . . .
Whether the two-way heart, the laughter
At little things would please you, John; the waiting
For louder nightingales, for the first flash and thunder
Of our awakening would frighten you—
I wonder sometimes, wishing for your company
This summer; watching time's contempt
For such as you and I, the daily progress
Of couch-grass on a wall, avid as death.
But you had courage. Facing the open fields
Of immortality, you drove the coulter
Strongly and sang, not marking how the soil
Closed its cut grin behind you, nor in front
The jealousy of stones and a low sky.
Perhaps, then, you'll accept my awkward homage—
Even this backyard garland I have made.

II

I'd give you wild flowers for decking
Your memory, those few I know:
Far-sighted catseye that so soon turns blind
And pallid after picking; the elder's curdled flowers,
That wastrel witch-tree; toadflax crouching
Under a wall; and even the unpersistent
Windflowers that wilt to rags within an hour . . .
These for a token. But I'd give you other
More private presents, as those evenings
When under lime-trees of an earlier summer
We'd sing at nine o'clock, small wineglasses
Set out and glittering; and perhaps my friend
Would play on a pipe, competing with the crickets—
My lady Greensleeves, fickle as fine weather
Or the lighter-boy who loved a merchant's girl.
Then we would talk, or perhaps silently
Watch the night coming.
Those evenings were yours, John, more than mine.
And I would give you books you never had;

29

The valley of the Loire under its pinewoods;
My friend Tom Staveley; the carved stone bridge
At Yalding; and perhaps a girl's small face
And hanging hair that are important also.
I'd even give you part in my shared fear:
This personal responsibility
For a whole world's disease that is our nightmare—
You who were never trusted nor obeyed
In anything, and so went mad and died.
We have too much of what you lacked.
Lastly, I'd ask a favour of you, John:
The secret of your singing, of the high
Persons and lovely voices we have lost.
You knew them all. Even despised and digging
Your scant asylum garden, they were with you.
When London's talkers left you, still you'd say
You were the poet, there had only ever been
One poet—Shakespeare, Milton, Byron
And mad John Clare, the single timeless poet.
We have forgotten that. But sometimes I remember
The time that I was Clare, and you unborn.

III

Whether you'd fear the shrillness of my voice,
The hedgehog-skin of nerves, the blind desire
For power and safety, that was all my doubt.
It was unjust. Accept, then, my poor scraps
Of proper life, my waste growth of achievement.
Even the cold eye and the failing hand
May be acceptable to one long dead.

12th–13th July 1941.

Neutrality

HERE not the flags, the rhythmic
Feet of returning legions; nor at household shrines
The small tears' offering, the postcards
Treasured for years, nor the names cut in brass.
Here not the lowered voices.
Not the drum.

Only at suppertime, rain slanting
Among our orchards, printing its coded
But peaceful messages across our pavements.
Only the cryptic swift performing
His ordered evolutions through our sky.
Only the growing.

And in the night, the secret voices
Of summer, the progression
Of hours without suspense, without surprise.
Only the moon beholds us, even the hunting owl
May watch us without malice.
Without envy.

We are no cowards, we are pictures
Of ordinary people, as you once were.
Blame not nor pity us; we are the people
Who laugh in dreams before the ramping boar
Appears, before the loved one's death.
We are your hope.

16th July 1941.

For M.C., *written in the train*

SICK travelling day, this day unravels
Landscapes and hopes like wrack; and listen
How the wheels race like suns in a steel heaven.

Day between days and given neither
To you nor me, the limbo of our loving;
This day will steal your face, and fasten
A mask of wire around my eager looking.

Forgive each wheel its gesture of repulsion;
And hope that I may sometime find direction;
That we may live at last under a quiet sun
Where no trains but God's sure thoughts need run.

29th July 1941.

Extracts from 'A journey through Limbo'

I

OVERTURE

(i)

AN old hand writing in frost
This epitaph may only write, this grief
Inscribe of wanderers and justify.
Only the moving hand of God will dare
Remember them, only the eye of time
Picture them, not my poor endeavour—
A child of their own sickness, without comfort.
Three were there. Two were lovers and ensnared
In all love's subterfuge of fire and folly;
Dark-haired and generous, pitifully young
She and her lover lived their fable bravely
And made their peace. The other,
Broken in youth, her brother, scarred
By all pain's ways and eaten hollow

As a gourd by pride, scored their fine dreams
With his hard impotence. He was a poet.
These three, then, creatures not of time but shaming
Time and the age's cruelty, my children
And teachers also, take, to learn
Their sorrow and their journey, hoping only
They may remain your friends; their suffering
Become your comfort, their travail be your book.

(ii)

The hand writes and the words stand
Bright as glass. There was a country . . .
And it is in your heart. There was a city . . .
A grey town by the sea, distracted
By the grey goose-skeins westward figuring
The sky and filled with their wild calling.
It is the town of autumn. You remember
Those skies and cries, all its directions.
There was a girl . . .
She's in you when you look at the east
Or when you dream of woods and a forgotten
Country of waters; when you smell the soil
In autumn; when you taste the red
Sharp berries of October. There was a fear . . .
Over that country, the grey town and the girl
And it is ours. The visual fear
Of mirrors which breaks thought; the fear
Of knives which splits the mind; the cold distrust
Of living which spells love. They came together
These fears one summer when a great man took
Power like a sickness, losing himself in power.
Fear ate at every place, immodest
Sly watcher in the mind. Fear grasped
The girl and stripped her without pity.
Fear paralysed all striving; shook the strong
And broke the weak, only could never
Subdue the writing hand.
None may deflect, none may subdue the hand.

Sometimes they'd see, the dark girl and the young
Lover she had, another and disquieting
Future behind the face of days; they'd think
Of others who failed, though young and good and lovely
Under the fear; and she would see no hope
For the hard man her brother, never quiet
Nor to be silenced, enemy of talkers,
Friend only to the dead, a crying voice.
And she would fear for him and fear him, knowing
His words were stronger than his enemies,
His will the weapon of the writing hand.
Break may the instrument, never fails the hand.
So he spoke out two years, grew hated slowly
By the great, feared by his fellows, loved
By her alone, supported by the hand.
Until the cruel watcher drew his knife
Which maims though never halts the hand.
                              And struck.

II

SPEECH BY THE COMPANION

Well may you think, you lovers, love no anguish
But breaking of the fine-tipped willow buds;
And the growth of love to lonely seekers
Of each not time's delight as fair
As Easter flowering of the palm. But Easter.
Well may you walk through fear
Shielded by folly, by the glances caged
Of adoration, well forget the saw-marks
Which eat the willow-tree and build the cross.
Well may you listen, lovers, to the snoring
Of nighted cities replete with the tears of the lonely:
For loneliness need stare at you no longer
Like an envious bloodshot eye. No longer
The ghosts of the lonely and the mad perform
Their shadow play behind your windows—
Two are not lonely. Never forget the third.
Well may you know his anger sprung
Before your step, a gin. His misery

Thick in your kisses, damning them. His pride
A hard-voiced bird singing its heart away
In your love's branches, in your hope's green wood.
Remember too the fourth, your cruel teacher,
The watcher with the knife, the saboteur;
Who is not bribed, never by lovers hired
Nor even by the wicked, though sought out
By the plain woman and the crook-backed king
And the conquerer who cannot kill his mind.
Never to leave you now. I am your devil.
Four walk through limbo. Three will not return.

August 1941.

William Wordsworth

NO room for mourning: he's gone out
Into the noisy glen, or stands between the stones
Of the gaunt ridge, or you'll hear his shout
Rolling among the screes, he being a boy again.
He'll never fail nor die
And if they laid his bones
In the wet vaults or iron sarcophagi
Of fame, he'd rise at the first summer rain
And stride across the hills to seek
His rest among the broken lands and clouds.
He was a stormy day, a granite peak
Spearing the sky; and look, about its base
Words flower like crocuses in the hanging woods,
Blank though the dalehead and the bony face.

September 1941.

Pheasant

COCK stubble-searching pheasant, delicate
Stepper, Cathayan bird, you fire
The landscape, as across the hollow lyre
Quick fingers burn the moment: call your mate
From the deep woods tonight, for your surprised
Metallic summons answers me like wire
Thrilling with messages, and I cannot wait
To catch its evening import, half-surmised.
Others may speak these things, but you alone
Fear never noise, make the damp thickets ring
With your assertions, set the afternoon
Alight with coloured pride. Your image glows
At autumn's centre—bright, unquestioning
Exotic bird, haunter of autumn hedgerows.

September 1941.

The glass tower in Galway

I

ONE was an eye and others
Snake-headed travesties; one high-legged and mincing
As a stork. And there were whining small ones
Like sickly children. O they were a beastly
Sea-born race, spawned on the rocks of Galway
Among the dried shark-eggs and the dirty froth.
They moved and cried and the wind blew hard from the West,
Ruffling the treacherous pale places over the reefs.
They cried, 'Ours is the land,'
And the gulls dared not dispute them
Nor even the old falcon circling the misty cape.
They took the crooked fields and straggling coasts
Of Galway, spreading later East and South
Through heather-topped hills and the stinking bogs of Connaught,
To caper lastly on the inland pastures
Where only the moon and the waving grasses mocked them.
But where the sea had retched them up

They built a tower, above the cross-grained tides
And wheezing potholed beaches, on a headland;
Of glass they reared it, riveted askew,
Sustained by witchcraft; in the autumn gales
Ringing like a goblet till the mountains quivered.
It was their shrine, and cruel sea-rites
Went forward there while they possessed the land:
Sometimes it shook with screaming and children's corpses
Drifted southward, mauled by the grumbling seals.
Yet still on summer nights impassively
It faced the empty West with its inane transparency.

II

But as the inhuman years neared their completion
A race came from the South; sun-bronzed
Cloud-riding Danaan people out of Egypt.
And there were battles. First among the ravaged
Hills and then raging by the stony beaches.
Wars passed; the sea took many dead, the tower
Fell and its rites were celebrated
Now only in the deep sea caverns where its masters
Sought refuge; now the fretful tide
Coughed round those altars without sacrifice;
Outlawed by history, the sea-born race
Rotted off Galway, the Atlantic shark
And groping spider-crab their only heir.
Those reefs and beaches now lay shadowless
Under the moon; the wheeling falcon saw
A new age coming, like the early sun
Gilding the spindrift, bronze on the wet sand.

III

But even that age is dead and songs
Forget its buried kings who lie
Under high cairns, their requiem the curlews'
Insatiable crying, their epitaph
In lichens written, and great deeds engraved
On buried shards of bronze. For history
Despises even them, turning their prowess
Into a tale of ogres, fame and truth
Lost in the wreck of their enormous bones.

IV

Bats roost in the high white halls
And the heroes are finished

Their swords are stacked for scrap
In the cold waste places.

Their tombs scattered and broken
Nourish the blue thistle.

For time will never repent
Nor the seasons pity them.

There's no hope in hoping now:
God has left us like a girl.

September 1941.

A letter from Tartary

'YOU will remember now our ways; know not
The seasonal journey to the broken shrine.
The going south in autumn too, no use
To wish for that, or for the singing rowers
Bending their backs in time with your own heart.
Hope not to stand again as then
In the ship's golden prow, chrysanthemums
Never more full of fire than your young face—
You can be pale as clay for all I care.
Look now, I'm sending you the only
Token my broken heart can spare, a ring
Set with a reptile's eye, the poor and only
Symbol my straying mind can find. A dragon
Once wore it, girl; blue and unpitying
Eye of his malice, in a mountain lake.
They trapped him with a kid, tore out those eyes
And let him starve. Wear it until you die
And say to every man you take, "A silly singer
Put this cracked sapphire on my finger;

38

A harebrained king gave me this ring. Beware."
Don't look for me. I've gone to meet the winter
By the long wall. A hard wind whips my face
Already loaded with the bitter sand
Of Tartary. My eyes are weak. Forget
The songs I made you, the coloured supple dancers,
The junketings and lanterns, the pale leaves
Of maple falling in the night, the night
You sang to a guitar and wildered me.
The torch stinks and the tent is
Full of smoke, the camels cough and strain . . .
But think when you're alone—you've lost a poet,
Made a king mad, driven a man frantic . . .
You won't forget our days any more than I:
I wish I had you still, I wish you dead
And cannot rest for hating you. O lovely . . .
Think of my end and be sick in your bed.'

It is a long way back and a long way
To where I'd be. Time will not pass. I've grown
Old since this journey started, and my mind
Will not stay still. O could I only turn
Back to those curious gardens, palaces
Of jade, and courtyards, stand by the carven gate
And find my girl there, neither proud nor unwilling.

September 1941.

Don Juan in winter

WHERE once it was under archways
The legendary two-backed beast and bright
As younger years the moonlight, dog-legged shadows
Hunting not then, sparing your hopeful night:

Now they run loose about the traitor streets,
You see in archways waiting the wronged man
You spitted, and the beast run down and cornered
Can only howl, harder its hunting than

The shame and terror of its own past quarry,
The cry at midnight. Now the hunt is up
For every dealer in expensive passion
And every drinker from the jewelled cup.

Alone in winter now, you dare not loiter
Along old ways, beside the terraced shore:
Your steps avoid the high-wrought palaces
Whose keys your fingers were, but are no more.

It is not vengefully nor yet in wisdom
You're punished so. The night will never fail;
But pretty faces fall and fail and never
Escape from their tired mirrors. Years as pale

As shipwreck are your portion, you once diver;
Once hunter, hunting. Serenaded windows yawn
Satirically like old gap-toothed women,
And age's dunghill cock crows up your dawn.

September 1941.

All Souls: A dialogue

I

TO MY FRIEND: J.H.S.

NOT early nor without questioning
The landscape clears; seek not the cold
Dew in the fields, nor go beguiled, my friend
Into rank thickets by its eager eyes.
Avoid the autumn birds that sing
Like brain-fever among the old
Defiant oaks; and at the pasture-end
Don't listen to the waking owl that cries
Long past his time and contradicts the sun.
Nature has plans against your peace of mind—
You must be cunning with her. When the wind
Cries like a child, sit behind bolted doors;
At All Souls feed the dead and shun
The drinking menhir on the midnight moors.

II

THE STRANGER

O otherwise than gently
The wind blows in your country.
I am the unborn lonely
Image of your destiny.

No portent goes before me,
No star; no virgin bore me.
But you dare not deny me
Conjure nor defy me.

You may not tip the arrow
With silver, exorcise me;
You may not pluck the yarrow
Against me, set the mask
At your heart's door, despise me
Or refuse what I ask.

III
THE REPLY

At the sad hour of twelve, the proper season
Had you come then, I should have known you:
Fear fails without its myth and reason
Avoids your face by day and will not own you.
A child, you were my other voice, your wisdom
Knew never season till my pride invented
Ways of defrauding you, contented
To make the hand my friend and time my home.

But now since time has failed me and forgetting
Its skill the hand, still impotent to pray,
Has left me maimed among the wheels and fingers
Of an ingenious age, teach me the way
To praise and love again before I'm shutting
My ears against the hours where your voice lingers.

IV
ADMONITION

Those evenings when summer mounted
The narrow stairs, and from the dead
Men's garden crept the tender promises
Of lilac in the night to turn my head:
I knew you then and jealously I counted
The moments for your coming. Or I said
'This is the time,' and then you'd let me call
Your names and seek you till the standing tower
Struck twelve and I went hopelessly to bed.
So now you've taken me entirely, meagre
Cramped house for such as you, and now mist rises
From fallen gardens, do not change or fall.
Be the vain lilac fresh for rain, so eager
To rot and fade. Do not forget that flower.

V
THE MESSAGE

Make love another language
Before the lean nails eat
Man's handed heritage
And fix in pain the mountain-walking feet.

The true speakers are dead,
Cracked in the valley of hate
The bones Ezekiel made
Articulate.

Love be your voice, voiceless
Millions and scattered bones:
Sing love, closed mouths of earth—
Hard is the singer's birth
But sing before the noiseless
Enemy comes.

VI
TO MY FRIEND: J.D.A.

Because of the cities they left, the roads
They drove into resisting continents:
Because of megaliths, impossible loads
Of stone yet reared by men, the builders live
Secure, earth's features now their monuments.

But earth must fall and falling races give
No thought to buried kings or marble lovers:
The archaeologist must follow with
His spade and ruler, and the fool discovers
The future not the founder's death in tombs.

So let's not advertise the immemorial
Autumn of flesh; let's cheat the easy provers
Of history's malice, build in human rooms
Our fame, in falling hearts our vast escorial.

September 1941.

Time will not grant

TIME will not grant the unlined page
Completion or the hand respite:
The Magi stray, the heavens rage,
The careful pilgrim stumbles in the night.

Take pen, take eye and etch
Your vision on this unpropitious time;
Faces are fluid, actions never reach
Perfection but in reflex or in rhyme.

Take now, not soon; your lost
Minutes roost home like curses.
Nicolo, Martin, every unhoused ghost
Proclaims time's strange reverses.

Fear was Donne's peace; to him,
Charted between the minstrel cherubim,
Terror was decent. Rilke tenderly
Accepted autumn like a rooted tree.
But I am frightened after every good day
That all my life must change and fall away.

2nd October 1941.

Lover's complaint

I
NOCTURNE

THE trains cry and are frightened
Far from my distraction; spare
My peace, my voice, my city
Of desolation, desolate because you are there.

There was a month and two people walked in it
But were not you or I:
My sight is broken and the signs are taken
That kept me safe in abject poetry.

Spare too my willing mind
That served your images:
There is a night and two people lie in it,
And the green planet rages.

Were I to pass now on the creaking stair
You would not know my face:
The months and the night and my own mind
Have taken a ghost's grace.

For my private streets and summers
Are any alien comer's;
And the tall miraculous city
That I walked in will never house me.

II
AUBADE

O sing, caged lark, sing caged
Poetical bird, you liar;
Sing high to-day, your female
Rapture, your cagebird fire
Won't fool me now, the day's already aged
Ten years and your voice falls stale.

O sing, erotic season, sing
Dream-heavy mind;
Light's terrible ministry
Perform, clear morning wind.
But my ears have aged and everything
Has turned round wretchedly.

October 1941.

A Renunciation

STRONG angels bear God's canopy,
Strong horsemen ride the loose immoderate wind:
But O my dark girl from her balcony
Laughs down and puts their glory out of mind.

Sharp stars are wiser than the astronomer,
The stinking goat more potent than the great
Lover of girls, that cold Casanova:
And righteous wars forget the cause of hate.

The high djinn-master Solomon
Could never understand his women's talk:
So I would be an unobservant man
Frequenting gardens where dark women walk.

October 1941.

Holstenwall

WE'RE going to the fair at Holstenwall;
It is my eyes you've taken out—
My bright eyes and my hollow heart
Stare and ring at Holstenwall.

I stand up straight, strong master, stand
Straight as a man, and am no man:
My pulses beat, O master, yet
I can help nothing. This is a wicked land.

Standing and stiff, send me forth, send
My fear forth, master. Cold boards hamper
My fingers, master, that would grope and clamber
Precise as spiders, grope and rend.

Swift and desiring, master, as a hound.
Let me get life, strong master, tear and wound
These dead crowds into life. O set
My course at this loud land, speed my swift feet.

Set me against the lover and the pope—
I need the living heart, the holy knowledge.
Give me the frightened girl and I will rape
Her life alive and cross the guarded bridge.

We're going to the fair at Holstenwall.
Remember your puppet: life lies in my hand:
Yet no dead doll or clockwork nightingale.
Have pity, master. This is a wicked land.

October 1941.

47

The bards

NOW it is time to remember the winter festivals
Of the old world, and see their raftered halls
Hung with hard holly; tongues' confusion; slow
Beat of the heated blood in those great palaces
Decked with the pale and sickled mistletoe;
And voices dying when the blind bard rises
Robed in his servitude, and the high harp
Of sorrow sounding, stills those upturned faces.

O it is such long learning, loneliness
And dark despite to master
The bard's blind craft; in bitterness
Of heart to strike the strings and muster
The shards of pain to harmony, not sharp
With anger to insult the merry guest.
O it is glory for the old man singing
Dead valour and his own days coldly cursed.

How ten men fell by one heroic sword
And of fierce foray by the unwatched ford,
Sing, blinded face; quick hands in darkness groping
Pluck the sad harp; sad heart forever hoping
Valhalla may be songless, enter
The moment of your glory, out of clamour
Moulding your vision to such harmony
That drunken heroes cannot choose but honour
Your stubborn blinded pride, your inward winter.

October 1941.

Against divination

NOT in the night time, in the weary bed
Comes wisdom, neither to the wild
Symbolic leaf of autumn. Never seek
Your solace from the automatic hand
Of medium, or lover's partial gaze:
Truth is not found in book or litten glass
At midnight. Ghosts are liars. None may turn
Winter's hard sentence but the silly man,
The workless plowman or the unhoused poet
Who walks without a thought and finds his peace
In tall clouds mounting the unbroken wind,
In dry leaves beating at the heavens' face.

Against a second coming

1
SPRING NIGHT

SPRING night, the owls crying
From copse to copse and the dew rising.

Then wonderful the empty field and waiting
For another people to be returning
From the dark rain and the jealous forest
Into their rest.

Still be that pathless place of comfort
And fair the flowering they sought:
Even the long-eared grasses in compassion
Ceasing their talk of scythe and resurrection.

Wise be the woods, and every pale-throated
Primrose at peace, you undevoted:
Cunning the river as your subtle thoughts
Turning a stone to blue or black-eyed quartz.

Unmoved the leaf, light lie the soil about
The fierce endeavour of the root:
Come not with your unquiet voice
Bidding the solitude rejoice.

Never so quiet be eye and grief
Though bone its panacea receive
Blood calls to blood and humours wrap
The tortuous runway of the sap.

O leave us, you lover, cease telling
Of sorrow past our healing:
Sleep and cease crying, you wounded
Against the undefended.

Spring night, plovers calling
Over the fallow and the dew falling.

II
THE WALKING WOMAN

There's a hard wind yet and a sad road
Between the walking woman
And her deadly spouse, the iron lover.
O my hair has fallen and my man
Has fallen and my fruitful time is over:
There is a hard wind and a sad road.

There's a jangled verse, a cry
Beating behind that woman's face.
O my eyes are drowned and my man
Is drowned. Who loves a dead man's grace,
A drowned man's kisses or a blind man's eye?
Cries the unsatisfied, the walking woman.

There's all the angry air, the sea,
Between that woman and her hope:
O once I had a house, a fire
Until my man's proud faring broke
My house and heart. So I'll desire
Lovers of iron or dead men's constancy,
Cries the still passionate, the walking woman.

III
THE LOVER

One stands at the door, importunate:
He brings no lantern and his language late
For love by some two thousand years
Beats at our dull accustomed ears.
One cries, 'Open, house of hate.'
There is a star in his face,
Cyclopean searcher of our white disgrace.
His fingers are candles shining
Sharper than fear:
The wind blows through, the kennelled hound is whining.
One cries, 'Open, I am here.'
His teeth are nails, he's put
Over the threshold now his iron foot:
The house is taken by a beggar's ghost.
The lights burn blue, the watchdog cowers dumb.
The voice says, 'Your past is lost,
         I have come home.'

IV
THE WITNESS

Now I stand witness in my future's trial:
Broken my house, my brothers drowned,
The wandering crazed woman in my mind
Called, not I, the iron accuser.
Yet stand I must, damnation fall
Upon the loveless loser.

The spring is my defence, before
The judge grew savage or the lover came;
I turned the year against them eagerly.
It was her lust, it was the woman's blame
Who would not rest, but opening the door
Betrayed the house by her false constancy.

I witness, then, she took my power,
Else had my word prevailed;
My strength is stolen, my defence has failed.
Soldier outplanned, snared eagle, I'm the loser;
A sorcerer prisoned in a quaking tower.

Regard my innocence, accuser.

V

THE CROWNING

Condemned and crowned, lay his bones proudly
Among the great betrayed.
Let his high head be laid
Easily down, prevent his avid enemy.

Nisus the eagle was he: crown
His brow with eagle's height.
Constantine the founder: turn
Attila from his gate.

Condemned and crowned, lay his bones easily.

Bind with the iron laurel that defeated
Notorious brain, that undefended head.
Lay him down easily, his testament completed,
His city taken and his brothers dead.

Condemned and crowned, lay him down easily.

The crown he wears is stronger than the bones
Of the illustrious; and by his side
His sword lies broken. Now he owns
The iron acanthus and the eagle's pride.

Condemned and crowned, lay his bones easily.

Meeting the iron lover in the door
He knew betrayal; yet unscared and eager
Though he'd defied the cruel season's power
He welcomed his accuser like a beggar.

Condemned and crowned, lay him down easily.

No wild involuntary woman
Shall trouble him; no goldfinch hover
Above his grave; nor shall this man
Be judged by Minos, prince of hell;

52

Nor his defended spirit dwell
In the dark rain of spring—
Condemned and crowned and triumphing
Against the cruel lover.

February—October 1941.

Glaucus

THE various voices are his poem now.

Under the currents, under the shifting lights
Of midway water, rolls his fleshy wreck:
Its gurnard eye reflects those airy heights
Where once it noted white Arcturus set.

Gull-swift and swerving, the wet spirit freed
Skims the huge breakers. Watching at the prow
Of any southbound vessel, sailor, heed
Never that petrel spirit, cruel as pride.

Let no cliff-haunting woman, no girl claim
Kinship with Glaucus, neither sow
The tide with daffodils, nor call his name
Into the wind, for he is glorified—
And cold Aegean voices speak his fame.

November 1941.

Troll Kings

O wake them not, the big-boned kings,
The sleepers and the sworded kings; the lonely
Inhuman kings who sit with drawn-up knees
Waiting with twisted eyes the time of terror.
O wake them not, the troll kings, the forgotten.

Seraphion the sleeper turns a tired
Metallic eyeball through the lacunae
Of the black tomb; and Arthur mumbles
The names of white-haired women, Guenever
Remembers, and her exhumation, bursting
Like a deep-buried mine on Avalon's touchy climate;
Lancelot too, the double lover, sees him
Riding the roads but rusty now his manners
And gaunt the horse, and white the horse he rides;
And the neurotic banners, and the guessed-at
Grail that was white and gracious as his hope.
Ragnar sleeps too, the great-sworded
King of the trolls, his language no more spoken
Now in the woods, except by winking squirrel
And furtive jay; lies battened
Under black rocks unknown to mole or miner.
Ragnar the ironmaster, O remember
Ragnar regretting the plump peasant girls
Who knew his kingdom and forgot the light.
So sleep the old troll kings, with Barbarossa
Who died on the sharp ice; with Attila
The Tartar buried in a northern forest;
With Alexander, the cold fugitive
From fame and politics; with all outmoded heroes.

O do not speak to them lest they rise up
One cold night under the moon to fight for us.
They wait a backward day: how should they know
Such folly as we suffer, such perplexity
Of soul, such deadly love, such wonder?
Then let them sleep, the poor things, this cold night.

November 1941

The island city

FOR R. J. S.

WALKING among this island
People inhabiting this island city,
Whose coast recedes, whose facile sand
Bears cold cathedrals restively:
I see a black time coming, history
Tending in footnotes our forgotten land.

Hearing the once-virginal
But ageing choirs of intellect
Sing a psalm that would appal
Our certain fathers, I expect
No gentle decadence, no right effect
Of falling, but itself the barren fall:
And Yeats' gold songbird shouting over all.

November 1941.

Schiller dying

WHEN there were rules to break, when I
Was punished and rebelled; then one might build
Castles and cities out of history, or walk
In grassy countries; then perhaps might yoke
Even the shy unbroken horse
That grazes no known pasture, the iron-hooved
Pegasus even—spur him from the fair
Out of the clapping and the roaring lamps
And freak-shows into windy ways of joy.
Joy . . . that is important in a way
I cannot tell, somewhere quite other than
This drunken planet . . . there are choirs crying
Joy in my head . . . It was, of course, disguise:
Not joy, but something positive, the root
Of love, the keynote. These high voices find
The explanation I dared never seek

55

Outside the words; now my joy is becoming
Not joy, but ringing hoofbeats of the horse
I stole to ride those mountains; singing
Chainshot at Lützen . . . blood starts through my joy
And Eger threatens. Listen to Wrangel, listen
To Max the foreigner, the foxy prince
Who never knew it; stand immovable
Beside me, under Saturn stricken also—
Save me from fear and Venus, guard my joy.
But in the end they pulled you down, they struck
Swords in your holy flesh, as now in mine
Fear spreads like poison . . . once I was not afraid
To hide my meaning, once I could assert
'Joy is a spark from heaven,' never thinking
I lied: that joy was only the reverse
Of my consumption, of the angry blades
At Eger; or that pain's repeated
All over the world's body, like a scar.

My nose is red. Perpetually climbs
The sickness through my bones—a spiral fever
Searching the marrow. Winter is too long . . .
And joy has coarsened the great poet's face
That challenged winter once; and silly women
Who laughed at me, climb to his high-flown bed.
Joy has devoured that man. My nose is dripping
Just as he said it did; always a snivelling
Poor Württemburger poet, while he rules
A soft world's pleasure with his easy joy.
There was another word . . . now I may speak
More openly . . . there was a foreign girl
Came to our winter valley, but she left us
In spring without a word. Her name was never
Joy—but I never knew her name at all.
And I knew more than joy, the day I came
Hopeful to Weimar, looking for a sun
To warm my winter, with the Mannheim voices
Forgotten and far off, beyond the hills.
That was the moment, when the hard-shaved teachers
And mouthing dukes lost hold of me; when Goethe
Lifted me out of fear in his great hands.
But now he's frightened too; and I am drifting

Back to the cruel school, the uniform
Of uncomplaining earth; back to the fair
Unhorsed and haggard now, a clumsy ploughboy
Forgetting how he harnessed the wild horse;
Back to the theatre, to the open faces
Of the untutored, unregenerate crowd. . . .

Joy is waylaid and slain. It was my joy
They murdered on the Rhenish roads, and left
A wheezing red-nosed ghost to end the journey.
My joy is murdered, tumbled in the ditch
With Rousseau and Wallenstein, a black blood-welter.
Joy, my Adonis, rise; now I can meet you
Unmasked in all your violence, dry blood
Hanging about your eyes, your beauty punished.
You need not come disguised. I have learnt courage.
Your face is like my own, too sensitive
For its fulfilment, crossed with heavy weals
And scored by time's derision. And your voice
Is hoof and chainshot, choir and orchestra; the weeping
King in his chamber; Eckermann and Goethe
Preparing fame over the hock-glasses;
My own dry coughing . . . or it is the cranes'
Accusing scream, the wild thin voices
Of cranes denouncing my joy's murderers . . .
The meaning is not joy. Joy died. The word
Is freedom and the bleeding face is freedom.
Goethe has lost it. I am only free
Since my youth died. The cranes are crying
Freedom and pain, freedom and fame. . . . My fear
Has left me. I am ready to set out.

November 1941.

Little Drawda

UNDER the shaken trees, wait O unlucky
Returner, you rejected one:
There is no way of comforting you. Wait
Under the shaken trees and the clock striking one.

In the moon's wicked glitter linger now
You tired ghost:
You have no stance of safety but shift
In the moon's glitter, an uprooted ghost.

On this strong night, remain you lonely
Seeker beside me, though my heart is dumb:
We may together solve the unexpected
Secret of living, now that the clock is dumb.

November 1941.

The parrot

THE bird speaks right to-night; my talking bird
Of blood attacks his cage, shouting our secrets.
His wisdom slapdash, he announces
Interpretation crooked—old man Parrot
I'd never reckoned with; poor Skelton's bird
Hopping between the ribs, cocking an eye
Into the cavities of the nervous skull,
Tells lovely tales of Troy, or the old town
Lo-Chang, love's odd necropolis; and speaks
Awry of joy and fame, that poor man's grave—
That well-known epigram of painful wit.
Speak, bird. Speke parot. Speak, then,
Heart in the night from your elaborate
Cage of white ribs: cry and defy decorum.

November-December 1941.

The cruel solstice

TO-NIGHT the stranger city and the old
Moon that stands over it proclaim
A cruel solstice, coming ice and cold
Thoughts and the darkening of the heart's flame.

'Stand up,' speaks soul, 'let wisdom turn the time
Into an image of your day's despite';
O clever soul, we were born separate,
Held only in hard glance or studied rhyme.

'Sleep then, tired singer, stop the mouth
Of the unhappy month and take your rest.'
O cunning voice, I have not strength enough,
Being no stranger here, but uncouth guest.

So must I walk or falter by the wall
Wondering at my impotence
Of thought and action; at the fall
Of love and cities and the heart's false diligence.

To-night I cannot speak, remembering
For all my daily talk, I dare not enter
The empty month; can only stand and think
Of you, my dearest, and the approaching winter.

Branwen sailing to Ireland

Prelude: LAY your hand,
Lay your hand here
Upon the pivot of the turning year:
This Branwen's breast, the sea-pale stranger queen
Shall feel the ravisher's mercy cold and keen.

Lay your eye,
Lay your bright eye and lip
Upon the lodestone of the driving ship:
Then shall you bitterly Branwen's power know
The fair unsmiling myth that will not let you go.

Lay your dear hope,
Lay your desire and hope
In Branwen's arms as in a hangman's rope.
Cursed with great beauty, she sails to savage Ireland
Holding our hope and our doom in her hand.

Branwen: The sea's a wolf-pack hunting a vast plain.
Let me meet love or die, but never come home again.

I was born, I know not how, too beautiful for peace.
Speed me to the ravisher who brings my release.

It's hard to be a stranger, rejected by the humble.
When I pass, the boys hide, the old hags mumble.

Hard to be a brittle queen, petrified in fable.
Let me learn the woman's part and laugh at the King's
table.

Sometimes I hate my flesh, because my heart is dead.
Let me find salvation in the King's bed.

Evnissyen: A woman is naught
But chattel or slut:
Some come with gold,
Some are ready, some cold—

But I'm a proud man, a noble voyager,
A prince's peer and a king's procurer.

Branwen the Queen
Stands fair between
The straining masts.
Beauty fades, fame lasts—
And it's fame I'm after, to make a treaty
With death and oblivion to spare my posterity.

I care not a whit
For love or might.
Though she make the bed
I shall stand at the head.
My name shall convey, my pride shall guide her:
For I'm a throne-shaker, a marvellous ambassador.

The Bard: My eyes went out too soon
To speak of beauty, for I never saw
Branwen the Queen, who is the old world's wonder.
Yet, for that cause, I may perceive a law
In history's vague tumult, like a raddled moon
Luring the sea into false force and thunder.

Beauty and pain and pride sail in a ship together;
The wind blows fair, but who shall rule the weather?
I am an old man without love or light
Straining at my songs like a goat at his tether.
But better for Branwen's lovers had they never known
the light.

Sometimes it happens in Spring, or at the end
Of Autumn, a harsh humour spurs my blood
Until I cry for sight, and the season wrings
Salt tears from my dead eyes, and April sings
A finer song than mine. And yet it's said
The blind are wise and darkness is man's friend.

To the singer, then, give darkness:
To the gallant, a fine funeral;
Spare Branwen from her loneliness
And my song be her memorial.

December 1941.

61

Sonnet i.m. The Lady Elizabeth Hastings

'To love her was a liberal education.'

I thought not, nor surmised, my darling,
You would be leaving us for that rumoured land:
You who lived fables all the time and, smiling,
Mocked death like a bad joke you did not understand.

It is much harder, oh it must be harder
For the schooled shade in that unlettered region:
Please God, the chirping dead will hover
Harmless about you, bear no damp contagion.

Hard for your pupil lover, who can match
No living lustre with your swaddled face:
I had not guessed that my poor eyes must watch
So long to find you at the dancing-place.
But you will harrow purgatory, teaching
The dead some hint of your defiant grace.

The snow

THEY said, It will be like snow falling—
To-night a hollow wind beating the laurels,
And in the morning quiet, the laurels quiet,
The soft sky resting on the treetops and
The earth not crying any more.

I read it would be safe, like snow lying
Locked in a secret promise with the ground.
And the clear distances, the friendly hills
Would whisper, It is easy, easy as sleep
To the lost traveller frozen in the field.

But now it's come, how different without
Those reassuring voices. Now I face
The bright white glare of January, naked
Among the clashing laurels, while the earth
Stumbles and cries like any lonely lover.

January 1942.

The migrant

SLIMMER than thrush, the ringneck ousel
Haunts these black becks, recalling chalk-ribbed downs
You walk this month; the heavy wrack
Stumbling across them in the winter dusk;
The gulls' extended shadows on the turf;
A Hampshire naturalist seeking, noting
The flocks, the fluting birds, (was it indeed
Migration brought them, or mere Providence?)
The ringnecked birds in Autumn on those downs.
So by the millrace and the stony ridge
I look for something different, for a sign
That love has flown into another country,
Migrating from this frost—not, as I fear,
Frozen and starved. The quick bird calls
Thinly among the willows, and I think
Of spring and of that winter friend. O voice,
O bird-throat, bird-throat, you know not
My deeper fear of time, my silly hope
That spring may find us eager and unchanged.

January 1942.

The mad lady and the proud talker

'LADY, we knew a mountain country rising
To love's own passes, and your light feet spanned,
Mocking, the pale crevasses of that land.'
'Yes, I was once
The snow queen's sister, yet for you the guide
To those high ranges where wise angels hide.
Mistress of rocks I was and winter's daughter—
See, though, my hands by my spike-bearded father
Punished for living, riven into rock.
My head is full of the cold spring-water.'
'Lady, your eyes creep sideways like the rain
Glinting across a rockface, and your eyes
Once were my wonder.'

'O yes, O yes,
My eyes are ice. They lacerate and grind
The tender sockets. They are restless things.'
'Lady, there is a lovers' place
Where the stream-water shakes the hanging leaves
Of osier and sallow; and the air
Is kinder there to beauty.'
                              'Let me be
For I am queen of peaks, my lover
A green star is, hanging on my high head.'
'O lady, there are younger and less cold
Lovers down there than I or any star.
For there is growing: limb and love and season
Grow carefully and wither without pain.
The mind is not distracted and the hand
Plucks gratefully the string or flowering branch:
They sing there.'
                              'Up among the ice
I and my garland of hard stonecrop fare
As well as princes. Never near
My brittle heart dare venture you or any
Striver or talker or proud mountaineer.
I am the glass girl of a crazy tale
Distracted by a pebble's size
And every mountain's cringing littleness.
Your words growl in my brain like moving screes
Until I fear your talking and my pain.'
'I am quite lost again.'
'And I alone, proud man.'

January 1942.

The foreign gate

'Wunderlich nah ist der Held, doch den jugendlich Toten. ... Das plötzlich begeis-
terte Schicksal
Singt ihn hinein in den Sturm seiner aufrauschenden Welt.'

RILKE.

I

PILLARS of mist
Mark the gate,
Give passage to the mortal truant; guns
Salute the end of gold- or moon-led fighter;
Shrill shells and projectiles
Divide the prison air and call the discontented
Soldier from dreams of artificial hate.
Triumphal letters, Read O read my hopeful:
'Enter all lovers with the mouths you kissed
Hanging like bracelets on an arm of smoke
Or speaking with the yokel mouths of bells
Out of your panic at a foreign gate.'
Enter, then, soldiers, lovers to possess
The day of stranger suns
Which light the hero's and commander's fate.

There is a way:
Remember too the way
Of speaking without lips, you early dead.
The brother plucked out of a foreign sky
To lie in fields of wreckage and white marble—
He will remember easy speech again.
The long-houred day
Of freedom will return, and those who lie
Out in the starshine comfortless
Will find some small redress
In speaking clear where the vague spirits warble
From their white foliage of bone . . .
Some will remember:
Lost and powerless
Among the ribs and wreck of war, their words
Will rise to comfort all the thin-voiced dead
Inhabiting the written porch like birds.

II

See, I have made you a bridge; a trumpet
You may shame silence with; a slender dovecot
For your returning, pigeoned now with speech
Instead of Roman ashes.
                                    O my brothers,
My shy bird-throated compeers and my rapid
Talkers of youth, return.
Companion me, long-separated lovers
Unknown but welcome; fill the solitary
Tower of my mind with your high singing; seek
My ruined house, you bird-shaped passengers,
Cheated and eager far-sent messengers
Pass through the lovelocked gate to my bright lure.

I am the fabled and symbolic tower
Peopled with eagles, and the deadly
Bird-calling lighthouse in a storm of war.
I am the columbarium of winged
Souls, full of wind and windblown prayer.
O see, poor crazy frozen flyers
My refuge for you; travellers
Lost in confusion by a foreign gate,
My bridge for you; and voiceless speakers,
Cry through the trumpet of my fear and rage.

III

                                    Between two woods,
Between the forest of fire and the club-handed
Wood of hard ice, pace the forgotten
Lovers defrauded by despite and war
And frigid veins and jealous father-figures
And time and too much company and fear
And dreams and violence and separation
Who are my speakers first, the homing voices
Vocal in me, the images
That burn in me like seeds of climbing fire
In a damp chimney. These my client spirits.

The planets climb uneasily their spirals
Trailing cold fire across the stricken face

Of gored Adonis in his myrtle thicket;
And coupled like young hounds the spirits pace
Through the dead starshine hopelessly
To part before a glittering foreign gate.
These are the voices:
Here between fire and ice
Between the frost's pale foliage and the bright
Leaves of the fire, they call continually
Without expecting answer . . .
      'I was cold
But found the well a colder couch.'
       'And I
Was a horse-riding roarer who came down
Among the furze. O you of growing arms,
Tree-rooted woman with a winter sky
Behind your face, O shelter me . . .'
        'Remember
The slackened lutestrings in my father's house
And the deep mourning morning of my death
Who never should have died . . .'
       'It is not right
To grin so wide, my dearest, as the shroud grips fame
Or to be limned in grave-clothes . . .'
       'O remember
The words the wind took on the river
The speech the wind made at our wedding
And the wind's mutter in another wood. . . .'
They, ranting so, deceive each other:
They call unceasingly and never
Meet face to face or learn the final word.

But separation is not all.
The wise starwatcher notes the barbs that fall
On willing Danaë, and the hostile night
Becomes a house of comfortable light.
The meeting under elms, the walk . . .
    '. . . My hands are broken, my hands
Are helpless now to image you, my eyes
To hold you helpless . . .'
       And the easy talk
Between the rigid avenues of lime
Have different meaning in a different time.

Turn your back and all five senses lie ...
    ' ... How could you give so much to death
Who never gave me anything at all? ...'
The image alters, but can never die.
And separation cannot be complete
Though eager spirits pace and vainly call.

Give back the hands; but it is not enough.
Give back the crossbeam eye, the private word:
Yet silence trembles and the fire
Burns clear as peril through the blood.
The ravening soil clutches at foot and hand.
Cold branches scrape the cheek.
       'The gulls
Come inland from the marshes, scream and drift
Over my landlocked city. O remember
I have no easy manners and the winter
Has frozen my warm words ...'
     Give back the days
Of love's high summer even; with the calling
Birds in the woodland; glimmer on the stream
Of eddy and of oar-splash; roads as grey
As evening; give back the sunburnt face,
The easy manners, and the trodden grass
Under the hedge: these things are not enough.
The lovers weep. There is no rest or pity.
There is no summer in that landlocked city.

It may be easy at first
It may be growing or a way of thinking
Or even habit. But there's no escape.
No ease at last, only the cold attraction
Of steel and magnet. Then the separation
That cannot be complete;
The calling spirits that may never meet;
The shattered engine sabotaged by time;
The locked cogs sundered each from each—
Imperfect to the Greek or shaped
Subtly by Satan to the prudish Mani.
Whichever way, eternity is crying
Out of the cold, out of the fiery wood—
And never separate;

69

Bound in unlucky fate
To riven mind and tumult in the blood
They wander through my sleep and shame my speaking:
The green star weeps and glimmers through the wind.
There is no separation, but no meeting
Between the fire and ice.
                              The probing mind
Of poet cannot reach to comfort them;
Between the deadly trees they call and pace.
The young god never hears
And astral tears
Splinter like diamonds on his ravaged face.

                              IV

The moon is a poor woman.
The moon returns to weep with us. The crosses
Burn raw and white upon the night's stiff banners.
The wooden crosses and the marble trees
Shrink from the foreign moon.
The iron gate glitters. Here the soldiers lie.
Fold up the flags, muffle the soldier's drum;
Silence the calling fife. O drape
The soldier's drum with heavy crêpe;
With mourning weeds muffle the soldier's girl.
It's a long way and a long march
To the returning moon and to the soil
No time at all.
                    O call
The soldier's glory by another name:
Shroud up the soldier's common shame
And drape the soldier's drum, but spare
The steel-caged brain, the feet that walk to war.

Once striding under a horsehair plume
Once beating the taut drums for war
The sunlight rang from brass and iron;
History was an angry play—
The boy grew tall and rode away;
The door hung slack; the pale girl wept
And cursed the company he kept.
And dumb men spoke

Through the glib mouths of smoke;
The servile learned to strike
The proud to shriek;
And strangled in their lovers' lips
The young fell short of glory in the sand
Raking for graves among the scattered sand;
The tattered flags strained at the wind
Scaring the thrifty kite, mocking the dead.
But muffle the soldier's drum, hide his pale head,
His face a spider's web of blood. O fold
The hands that grip a splintered gun.
                    The glittering gate
Baffles him still, his starvecrow soul. O drape
The soldier's drum and cry, who never dare
Defy the ironbound brain, the feet that walk to war.

The cold hand clenches. The stupid mouth
Writhes like a ripple. Now the field is full
Of noises and dead voices . . .
                              'My rags flap
Though the great flags are trampled . . .'
                                  'My mouth speaks
Terror and truth, instead of hard command.'
'Remember the torn lace, the fine coats slashed
With steel instead of velvet. Künersdorf
Fought in the shallow sand was my relief.'
'I rode to Naseby' . . . 'And the barren land
Of Tannenberg drank me. Remember now
The grey and jointed corpses in the snow,
The struggle in the drift, the numb hands freezing
Into the bitter iron . . .'
                        'At Dunkirk I
Rolled in the shallows, and the living trod
Across me for a bridge . . .'
                            'Let me speak out
Against this sham of policy, for pain
Alone is true. I was a general
Who fought the cunning Africans, returned
Crowned with harsh laurel, frantically cheered
Through Roman streets. I spoke of fame and glory.
Women grabbed at my robe. Great poets praised me.
I died of cancer, screaming, in a year.'

'I fell on a black Spanish hillside
Under the thorn-hedge, fighting for a dream
That troubled me in Paris; vomited
My faith and courage out among the stones...'
'I was a barb of light, a burning cross
Of wood and canvas, falling through the night.'
'I was shot down at morning, in a yard.'

The moon regards them without shame. The wind
Rises and twitters through the wreck of bone...
                                    'It is so hard to be alone
Continually, watching the great stars march
Their circular unending route; sharp sand
Straying about the eyes, blinding the quick-eyed spirit.'
A soldier's death is hard;
There's no prescribed or easy word
For dissolution in the Army books.
The uniform of pain with pain put on is straiter
Than any lover's garment; yet the death
Of these is different, and their glory greater.
Once men, then moving figures on a map,
Patiently giving time and strength and vision
Even identity
Into the future's keeping;
Nourished on wounds and weeping
Faces and laughing flags and pointed laurels,
Their pain cries down the noise of poetry.

So muffle the soldier's drum, forget the battles;
Remember only fame's a way of living:
The writing may be greater than the speaking
And every death for something different
From time's compulsion, is a written word.
Whatever gift, it is the giving
Remains significant: whatever death
It is the dying matters.
                              Emblematic
Bronze eagle or bright banner or carved name
Of fighting ancestor; these never pardon
The pain and sorrow. It is the dying pardons,
For something different from man or emblem.
Then drape the soldier's drum

72

And carry him down
Beyond the moon's inspection, and the noise
Of bands and banners and the striking sun.
Scatter the soldier's emblems and his fame:
Shroud up the shattered face, the empty name;
Speak out the word and drape the drum and spare
The captive brain, the feet that walk to war
The ironbound brain, the hand unskilled in war
The shrinking brain, sick of an inner war.

V

Were I to mount beyond the field
Of battle and the lovers' wood to that high-pillared house
Where the great sit, in stone unmoved yet knowing
The world's minute catastrophes;
Judged yet unjudging, presences of fame
And still perfection; were I to speak out clear
In that high house, a voice of light might answer.
Once a man cried and the great Orders heard him:
Pacing upon a windy wall at night
A pale unlearned poet out of Europe's
Erratic heart cried and was filled with speech.
Were I to cry, who in that proud hierarchy
Of the illustrious would pity me?
What should I cry, how should I learn their language?
The cold wind takes my words.
                        What broad-winged eagle
Could bear me through this night, whose thoughts are
  pinioned?
No eagle now, for man's mind is divided
And the straight ways are shut, the singing
Voices are broken, there is only noise.
Yet knowing this, I will salute the presences,
Mounting a coward's stair.
                    The walls are harsh
To groping hands, under ascending feet
The smooth stairs twitter. Battle-noises mount
Behind me, and the grinning smoke
Hangs nooses in the air.
                  Pardon my coming
Who am not stone and have no final voice
To conquer chaos, neither sword nor laurel.

The gates are filled with mist; slow-turning pillars
Of cloud surround them. And beyond
Live death's great enemies, the undefeated.
These are a stronger nation. Death tried many
Ways to invade their citadel of mind,
Always in vain; until the mortal hour
When they at last let down the bridge and flung
The gates apart, but left no easy plunder.
A greater victory lay in that surrender.

They knew their enemy. His ambushes
Could not surprise them. Even separation
Meant nothing to their eyes, or changed their speech.
Maimed fingers, ebbing blood, the quarrelling of nerves
Could never frighten them; and broken armies
Were their continual triumph.
                                    Always came
The meeting in the myrtle-wood, escape
Between the slender trees, the rising
Of loved and lover into a clear sky;
Their images remaining in the lake
Like written words, the grateful air retaining
Their impress, like a dancer's or a bird's.

Wrestling with angels, they found out in time
Only the coward will resist that fall;
And so, embracing bravely the white limbs,
Engulfed in the long shining hair, they learnt
Humility and triumph.
                                    Some stretched out
Their hands to fire and calumny. Some ran
Upon the spikes of fear. Some lived for years
Alone with panic in a stuffy room
Until they grew good neighbours. Some were mad
Talking with flies and worms; and died for love
A double suicide without despair.
                                    These are the presences
Who sit beyond the gates, their heads as high
As towers in a dream, their silent faces
Unbitten by the frost, by rain unbeaten;
Their eyes like mirrors reinterpreting
The moon's distracted gaze, their strong hands folded.

Look in those eyes and learn the speech of pain;
Regard those hands, whose touch was clearer sight;
The stone lips curve, whose words were mountainous.
O my head I veil and turn my face to the wall
And pass from the place of wisdom's quiet children.
Their presence is a scroll of peace
Unrolled before the shattered face
Of the dead soldier and the straying lover.
I pass the shining gate
Into the unknown light
Of a low sun, knowing that death is conquered:
For the great have come home, whom all the clamour of history
Will never deafen or decrease their glory.

VI

Ruins and rocks cold and the starshine cold
Between these ruins.
I pass from the shadow-dance, the pillared house
Among these ruins.
The wind plays music and the moon returns:
The crosses stand like candles and the wood
Is full of crying.
            Spirits call and cower
Like light-crazed birds about the foreign gate.
Their speech is shrill, they whistle without lips;
Truth beats upon their narrow brain
With a thin ringing:
But gone like the lovers and the swift ships
Are the words of their singing.

The great have come home and the troubled spirits have spoken:
But help or hope is none till the circle is broken
Of wishing death and living time's compulsion,
Of wishing love and living love's destruction.
Till then, the soul is caged in brain and bone
And the observant man must walk alone.

Mirrors and white perspectives of despair
Surround the seeker:
Words pass like figures in a windblown fire;
The gabblings of unsatisfied desire
Confound the speaker.
This country of unfinished monuments

Troubles my vision:
It is well to remember the stone faces
Among these ruins.

February-March 1942

Simon Magus

THE hands affright, it is the cunning hands
Have driven my weak masters out of doors:
For a gold piece or healing water-kiss
Shaped like a cross, make my hands strong as yours.

The hand fails because of the unpurged eye.
The kiss fails because of the cold coin.
There is no power on earth can circumvent
The stubborn intellect, proud as a god's pain.

Go pray, Simon; hide your noisy heart
Clapper-tongued and lolling with conceit.
Meet your master in his house of fire
And practise wonders on the silly dead.
For you the mathematics of desire,
The frigid neophyte, the cold symbolic bed.

February 1942.

Early spring

NOW that the young buds are tipped with a falling sun—
Each twig a candle, a martyr, St. Julian's branched stag—
And the shadows are walking the cobbled square like soldiers
With their long legs creaking and their pointed hands
Reaching the railings and fingering the stones
Of what expended, unprojected graves:
The soil's a flirt, the lion Time is tamed,
And pain like a cat will come home to share your room.

March 1942.

Lament for Adonis

I bring you branches and sing scattering branches.
My feet have never turned this way before.
My tears are statues in my lighted eyes.
My mind is a stone with grief going over it
Like white brook-water in the early year.
I bring you tears and sing scattering tears.
My grief for you is cold and heavy as iron.
Your beauty was a wound in the world's side.

I bring you blood and sing scattering blood.

March 1942.

Hopes for a lover

I'D have you proud as red brocade
And such a sight as Venus made
Extravagantly stepping from a shell.

I'd have you clear your way before
With such a look as Aias wore
On his way back from hell.

I'd have you strong as spider's strand
And all volcanic as the land
Where the nymph fooled that cunning Ulysses.

I'd have you arrogantly ride
Love's flurry, as the turning seas
Bore Arion upon a fish.
My last and dearest wish—
That you should let the arrows of my pride
Come at you again and again and never touch you.

March 1942.

Lament for harpsichord: The flowering orchards

THE days and faces: O to take the faces
And crumbling features of my love and build them
Into a wall about our flowered April.
Rain seeks the root. The cloudy spring approaches.
If we could for a moment be alone,
Had it been possible for us to meet
Among the flowering orchards of the South
Or when the summer flashed and rocketed
Between green sedges like a kingfisher:
If we could be alone, my dear, my dearest,
With the pale light of April and the open
Roads of a tired heart, my far, my farthest,
There might be hope and heavy trees this summer
Instead of these hard blooms, this backward spring—
The gapped walls and the falling faces,
The scraggy birds that will not learn to sing.

Those flowering orchards, O to save those orchards
Of starred illusion from the climbing blight.
Silver it settles on the leaves and fissures
The strong bole slowly, to its circled heart.
If we could be alone for a moment only
While the spring grows, while blossoms fight
Within the bud. . . .
                                    If we had met before
And in another place, what wonders might we see
Sheltered by days and faces, under a flowering tree?

March 1942.

Medallion

BULL-CHESTED and iron-eyed heroes
And weeping women
Surround me while I sleep:
Waking, I meet the continual procession
Of hawk-headed, bird-clawed women
And weeping men.

March 1942.

78

Anarchy

RISING, the light ran round inside his eyes.
Then at a later hour, without surprise,
He noted singing birds that raked the sky
With pointed rods of sound like surgeons' knives.

The walls were scrawled with moss. The trees
Grabbed at the sun like grey anemones.
At noon he met a girl whose body sang
Thin as a cricket, till his eardrums rang.

Black dancers crossed his brain. The bearded sun
Whirled past him, locked with prancing Capricorn.
A dog began to howl, until he cried
It was too much. And then his wonder died.

Evening found him lost but unafraid
Surveying the wry landscape in his head.
Night ravished him, and so was brought to birth
A great cold passion to destroy the earth.

March 1942

War poet

I am the man who looked for peace and found
My own eyes barbed.
I am the man who groped for words and found
An arrow in my hand.
I am the builder whose firm walls surround
A slipping land.
When I grow sick or mad
Mock me not nor chain me:
When I reach for the wind
Cast me not down:
Though my face is a burnt book
And a wasted town.

March 1942.

To keep off fears

FEAR of jammed windows and of rising footsteps
Out of fear's stair, where a tall phantom mounts
Through time and action at the brain:

Fear of the enormous mountain leaning
Across thought's lake, where blinded fishes move
As cold and intricate as love:

Fear of the fisherman
Who raised Leviathan
On a steel line from his creative mirror:
Fear of the moonlight shifting against the door:

Fear finally of tripwire and garotte
Reaching possessive from an easy air:
These bring the careful man into despair.

Then let me never crouch against the wall
But meet my fears and fight them till I fall.

March 1942.

A hope for those separated by war

THEY crossed her face with blood,
They hung her heart.
They dragged her through a pit
Full of quick sorrow.
Yet her small feet
Ran back on the morrow.

They took his book and caged
His mind in a dark house.
They took his bright eyes
To light their rooms of doubt.
Yet his thin hands
Crawled back and found her out.

March 1942.

Ulster soldier

RAIN strikes the window. Miles of wire
Are hung with small mad eyes. Night sets its mask
Upon the fissured hill. The soldier waits
For sleep's deception, praying thus: O land
Of battle and the rough marauders lying
Under this country, spare me from my mind.
This year is blackened: as your faces blackened
Turn to the bedrock, let me not be rotted:
My limbs be never shackled in the roots
Of customary sin, as yours are bound
With oak and hawthorn. Spare me from my mind.
We come of a very old related race—
Drivers of cattle, kings, incendiaries,
Singers and callous girls; we know the same
Perplexities and terrors—whether to turn back
On the dark road, whether to love
Too much and lose our power, or die of pride:
The fear of steel, or that the dead should mock us—
These trouble our proud race. Protect me now.

The wind cries through the valley. Clouds sprawl over
This exiled soldier, sprawling on his bed.
Sleep takes the bartered carcase, not the brain.
It's only love could save him from his mind.

Omagh, 13th April 1942.

The true heart

SPA glints and quartz across the singing beaches
Of this volcanic island, the true heart:
Drowned bones above the tidemark show where seekers
For treasure fail, and lovers lie apart.

Those who land here, the restless and the lonely,
Lay down their fears at last in shifting graves:
The crippled spirit hides its long infirmity
Among the tangle of these crystal caves.

Guarded from love and wreck and turbulence
The sad explorer finds security
From all distraction but the thin lament
Of broken shells remembering the sea.

Omagh, 15th April 1942.

The vines are planted

(FOR J. H. S.)

THE vines are planted, but the wall is bare.
Two Autumns, in the warm reluctant soil
We set the man-shaped roots to cheer our Spring
Thinking no harm or false temerity:
But time knew better, withered up their rheum—
We cannot live upon posterity.

Planting and grafting, the young poet gropes
Through leaf and tendril to the failing root:
His eyes were full of sunlight and the Spring.
But love ceased falling and the worms grew bold.
His house was conquered by the arrow-weed:
He ran out howling in the winter cold.

The hand is writing, but the page is bare.
We are unthrifty vintners. We have raised
Great rootless gardens from our impotence
To challenge this unlovely season's envy:
So now they bloom across the bitter wind
Like the immortal spurge, the tempest's enemy.

May 1942.

Dunbar, 1650

THEY came down from the ridge.
Scarped hills swallowed them.
Under the walls grew spiked
Iceweed and bleeding men.

The preachers cried. Their gowns
Flapped among the wrack.
The lame general rode
Ashamed, with a bent back.

Crossing the little river
Their pikes jostled and rang.
The ditches were full of dead
A blackbird sang.

The southern terrible squire
Rode them down in the marsh.
The preachers scattered like crows—
The name of the day was WRATH.

June 1942.

Images of distress

THE old man ruinous upon the heath;
The young man mocking at a foreign court;
Instruct us in the ways of love and death—
Their images usurp our proper thought.

The lilac dreaming in the lover's garden:
The wild thyme splayed against the paving-stones
Are equal images of man's distress—
Their roots grope blindly for the lover's bones.

The wild gulls crying on the windy shore,
The dark-haired girl with summer in her face,
Silence the knocking stones inside my head,
Yet drive me out from every resting-place.

June 1942.

The uncreated images

THE commerce of lithe limbs is fool's delight.

O hours and watches, O unending summer
Within the lover's blood and cloudy blooms
That nightly rise and break about the body—
These are the currency of dreams and language,
The uncreated images of truth.

Night's wink is momentary, and dividing
The coloured shapes of passion which it spawned,
Night strikes through the membrane to the gristled socket
And tumbles like a pebble through the skull.

There is no speech to tell the shape of love
Nor any but the wounded eye to see it;
Whether in memory, or listening to the talk
Of rain among the gutters; or at dawn
The sentry's feet striking the chilly yard,
There is no synonym for love's great word—
No way of comforting the limbs
That have lain lovelocked at an earlier season,
Nor any coin to close the tired eye
That day chastises with its rod of light.
The separate limbs perform a faithless task—
The eye devours created images.

The commerce of lithe limbs is fool's delight
Cry limb and eyeball, waiting for the night.

Not chosen

(*FOR MILEIN*)

NOT chosen, but unsure protagonist
Of my father's folly and his father's greed,
I rake the acre that I should have sown
And burn the corn to save next season's seed.

Forgive my heavy hands their new precision
Learnt otherwise than we had wished or hoped;
Look not too closely as I move beside you—
My feet are shackled and my neck is roped.

I am the watcher in the narrow lane—
My tongue is schooled in every word of fear.
O take me back, but as you take remember
My love will bring you nothing but trouble, my dear.

July 1942.

Two Offices of a Sentry

I

OFFICE FOR NOON

AT the field's border, where the cricket chafes
His brittle wings among the yellow weed,
I pause to hear the sea unendingly sifted
Between the granite fingers of the cape.
At this twelfth hour of unrelenting summer
I think of those whose ready mouths are stopped.
I remember those who crouch in narrow graves.
I weep for those whose eyes are full of sand.

II

OFFICE FOR MIDNIGHT

The ones who gave themselves to every moment
Till time grew gentle as a sated lover;
The young swift-footed and the old keen-eyed,
Whose roads are freedom and whose stars are constant,
Stand by me as I watch this empty town.
I am in love with the wildness of the living.
I am in love with the rhythms of dead limbs.
I am in love with all those who have entered
The night that smells of petals and of dust.

July 1942.

Song: The heart's assurance

O never trust the heart's assurance—
Trust only the heart's fear:
And what I'm saying is, Go back, my lovely—
Though you will never hear.

O never trust your pride of movement—
Trust only pride's distress:
The only holy limbs are the broken fingers
Still raised to praise and bless.

For the careless heart is bound with chains
And terribly cast down:
The beast of pride is hunted out
And baited through the town.

July 1942.

Design for a monument

THE stone doves settle on the lady's tomb.

Grey scrolls of lettering upon her eyes
Will never hide the image of regret;
And she who walked in a rich robe of safety
Now shrinks beneath the rough immodest shroud.

O elegies are empty as the waiting
Of timid ancestors and scraping parents
Who worked so long towards that ruined face.
All walks at evening amongst the stolid yews,
And mornings at high windows, are forgotten
Like folds in a gold robe laid out to rot.
The lovers who rode with her lie scattered
Among their horses' big-eyed skulls in the meadow;
The yellow charlock scratches at her door.

It is not easy to lament a lady
Whose past was greater than the singer's age.
They who fly falcons at the angry sun
Or ride black horses through the armoured night
Have wept for her a day, then fallen sick
And laid their bones in cold heraldic houses:
And I am left to pause before her tomb
Where grey doves cover her with granite leaves.

July 1942.

Night estuary

AND yet the spiked moon menacing
The great humped dykes, scaring the plaintive seafowl,
Makes no right image, wakes no assertive echo.
Though one may stride the dykes with face upturned
To the yellow inflammation in the sky
And nostrils full of the living samphire scent,
There is no kindness in man's heart for these.
In this place, and at this unmeaning hour,
There is no home for a man's hope or his sorrow.

O you lion-hearted poet's griefs, or griefs
Wild as the curlew's cry of passage;
O hope uneasy as the rising ebb
Among the sedges, cold and questing guest:
Leave me alone this hour with the restive night.
Allow me to accept the witless landscape.

July 1942.

The gardener

IF you will come on such a day
As this, between the pink and yellow lines
Of parrot-tulips, I will be your lover.
My boots flash as they beat the silly gravel.
O come, this is your day.

Were you to lay your hand like a veined leaf
Upon my square-cut hand, I would caress
The shape of it, and that would be enough.
I note the greenfly working on the rose.
Time slips between my fingers like a leaf.

Do you resemble the silent pale-eyed angels
That follow children? Is your face a flower?
The lovers and the beggars leave the park—
And still you will not come. The gates are closing.

O it is terrible to dream of angels.

July 1942.

Orestes and the furies

This self-absorbed Orestes speaking riddles
Wanders the falling woods of his own past;
Remembering the pillared house, he weeps for
A mother murdered and a sister lost.

Of Agamemnon felled like groaning timber—
Alas the day he turned his back on Troy—
The hunted hero muses, and his mother
Who made him tremble like a lovestruck boy.

The mask of tragic pride upon his features
Is painted with inexorable art.
The guilty hands of mother and of sister
Are both the iron hand upon his heart.

Observing shapes of judgment in the sky
He seeks the dark, yet dare not turn his back
Upon those shattered mirrors where he sees
The snake-haired Furies running on his track.

July 1942.

Seascape

(FOR R.-J.)

OUR country was a country drowned long since,
By shark-toothed currents drowned:
And in that country walk the generations,
The dancing generations with grey eyes
Whose touch would be like rain, the generations
Who never thought to justify their beauty.
There once the flowering cherry grasped the wall
With childish fingers, once the gull swung crying
Across the morning or the evening mist;
Once high heels rattled on the terrace
Over the water's talk, and the wind lifted
The hard leaves of the bay; the white sand drifted
Under the worm-bored rampart, under the white eyelid.

Our country was a country washed with colour.
Its light was good to us, sharp limning
The lover's secret smile, the fine-drawn fingers,
It drew long stripes between the pointed jaws
Of sea-bleached wreckage grinning through the wrack
And turned cornelian the flashing eyeball.
For here the tide sang like a riding hero
Across the rock-waste, and the early sun
Was shattered in the teeth of shuttered windows.

But now we are the gowned lamenters
Who stand among the junipers and ruins.
We are the lovers who defied the sea
Until the tide returning threw us up
A foreign corpse with blue-rimmed eyes, and limbs
Drawn limp and racked between the jigging waves.

August 1942.

The Kestrels

WHEN I would think of you, my mind holds only
The small defiant kestrels—how they cut
The raincloud with sharp wings, continually circling
Above a storm-rocked elm, with passionate cries.
It was an early month. The plow cut hard.
The may was knobbed with chilly buds. My folly
Was great enough to lull away my pride.

There is no virtue now in blind reliance
On place or person or the forms of love.
The storm bears down the pivotal tree, the cloud
Turns to the net of an inhuman fowler
And drags us from the air. Our wings are clipped.
Yet still our love and luck lies in our parting:
Those cries and wings surprise our surest act.

August 1942.

Dido's lament for Aeneas

HE never loved the frenzy of the sun
Nor the clear seas.
He came with hero's arms and bullock's eyes
Afraid of nothing but his nagging gods.
He never loved the hollow-sounding beaches
Nor rested easily in carven beds.

The smoke blows over the breakers, the high pyre waits.
His mind was a blank wall throwing echoes,
Not half so subtle as the coiling flames.
He never loved my wild eyes nor the pigeons
Inhabiting my gates.   *August 1942.*

Figure of a bird and a ring

THE Phoenix rising in a storm of ashes—
O what wild tree shall bear the taloned singer?—
Grips in its serried beak my ring of power.
The reptile ash shall bear the Phoenix' pride.

The pale ash growing by the pool of eyes
Shall raise the golden-eyed heroic bird.
Be silent, nightingale, moss-haunting wren:
The Phoenix' cry shall haunt the summer wood.

And as that cry arises, so the ring
Falls spinning through the pool of frightened eyes;
And as the Phoenix rules the towering wood,
My ring lies rusting in a cell of quartz.
                                                       August 1942.

Rome remember

THE bright waves scour the wound of Carthage.
The shadows of gulls run spiderlike through Carthage.
The cohorts of the sand are wearing Carthage
Hollow and desolate as a turning wave;
But the bronze eagle has flown east from Rome.

Rome remember, remember the seafowls' sermon
That followed the beaked ships westward to their triumph.
O Rome, you city of soldiers, remember the singers
That cry with dead voices along the African shore.

Rome remember, the courts of learning are tiled
With figures from the east like running nooses.
The desolate bodies of boys in the blue glare
Of falling torches cannot stir your passion.
Remember the Greeks who measured out your doom.
Remember the soft funereal Etruscans.

O when the rain beats with a sound like bells
Upon your bronze-faced monuments, remember
This European fretful-fingered rain
Will turn to swords in the hand of Europe's anger.
Remember the Nordic snarl and the African sorrow.

The bronze wolf howls when the moon turns red.
The trolls are massing for their last assault.
Your dreams are full of claws and scaly faces
And the Gothic arrow is pointed at your heart.

Rome remember your birth in Trojan chaos.
O think how savage will be your last lamenters:
How alien the lovers of your ghost.

August 1942.

The doubtful season

THE doubtful season of the brain's black weather
Blew through me, but you waited for its end.
My months were all named backwards till you showed me
That even the mind is not deceived for ever.

O in October it would be the blazoned
Leaves of the chestnut on the cobbled pavement:
And we would seek in the corridors of autumn
Denial of faith and of the summer's achievement.

And in the early year it was another
Sign of evasion when the poplars clattered
To sharpened ears above the metal river—
And I would turn to find your eyes were shuttered.

Even that almost parting on the stair
I could not understand, nor why the candles
Sprouted such flowers between our sculptured faces:
Nor why the river glinted in your hair.

O in July it was our love was started
Like any hare among the watchful grasses;
Its running is my song, my only story
How time turns back and the doubtful season passes.

September 1942.

The promised landscape

(FOR R.-J.)

HOW shall I sing for you—
Sharing only
The scared dream of a soldier:
A young man's unbearable
Dream of possession?
How shall I sing for you
With the foul tongue of a soldier?

We march through new mountains
Where crows inhabit
The pitiful cairns.
At morning, the rock-pools
Are matted with ice.
But you are the mountains
And you the journey.

We lie in a ruined farm
Where rats perform
Marvels of balance
Among the rafters.
And rain kisses my lips
Because you are the sky
That bends always over me.

How shall I sing for you
Knowing only
The explorer's sorrow,
The soldier's weariness?
New ranges and river
Are never quite revealing
Your promised figure.

How dare I sing for you
I the least worthy
Of lovers you've had:
You the most lovely
Of possible landscapes?

September 1942.

99

Timoshenko

HOUR ten he rose, ten-sworded, every finger
A weighted blade, and strapping round his loins
The courage of attack, he threw the window
-Open to look on his appointed night.

Where lay, beneath the winds and creaking flares
Tangled like lovers or alone assuming
The wanton postures of the drunk with sleep,
An army of twisted limbs and hollow faces
Thrown to and fro between the winds and shadows.
O hear the wind, the wind that shakes the dawn.
And there before the night, he was aware
Of the flayed fields of home, and black with ruin
The helpful earth under the tracks of tanks.
His bladed hand, in pity falling, mimicked
The crumpled hand lamenting the broken plow;
And the oracular metal lips in anger
Squared to the shape of the raped girl's yelling mouth.
He heard the wind explaining nature's sorrow
And humming in the wire hair of the dead.

He turned, and his great shadow on the wall
Swayed like a tree. His eyes grew cold as lead.
Then, in a rage of love and grief and pity,
He made the pencilled map alive with war.

September 1942.

The poet

(*Translated from the German of Rainer Maria Rilke.*)

THE hour slips from me: wingbeats of the hour
Wound me and take my peace away.
I am alone. Yet what strange power
Inhabits all my life, my night, my day?

Unhoused and loverless I live
In no sure place, lacking all centre:
I give myself and as I give
Possess the world by that surrender.

The expected guest

THE table is spread, the lamp glitters and sighs;
Light on my eyes, light on the high curved iris
And springing from glaze to steel, from cup to knife
Makes sacramental my poor midnight table,
My broken scraps the pieces of a god.

O when they bore you down, the grinning soldiers,
Was it their white teeth you could not forget?
And when you met the beast in the myrtle wood,
When the spear broke and the blood broke out on your side,
What Syrian Veronica above you
Stooped with her flaxen cloth as yet unsigned?
And either way, how could you call your darling
To drink the cup of blood your father filled?

We are dying to-night, you in the aged darkness
And I in the white room my pride has rented.
And either way, we have to die alone.

The laid table stands hard and white as to-morrow.
The lamp sings. The West wind jostles the door.
Though broken the bread, the brain, the brave body
There cannot now be any hope of changing
The leavings to living bone, the bone to bread;
For bladed centuries are drawn between us.
The room is ready, but the guest is dead.

September 1942.

Epithalamium

(For R. B. and H. S.)

O you will have no bells and the winter is coming,
But now the corn lies down to the stumbling thresher,
The sycamore drops its yellow-winged projectiles
And winter is coming, but first the season of fruit.

Your bells will be the voices of autumn rivers,
Yout wine will be the dew on the fallen apple:
I sing for you who at the end of summer
Have crowned the year and come together at last.

There's so much burning in the autumn world.
The flames spread through the stubble, and the wind
Comes out of Russia with a smell of fire.
The reapers do not sing, but the sickle whispers
Among the leaning wheat in the heat of noon.

O you have seen, as I have seen, the folly
Of those who think lost time can be repaid:
The girl who, mad with sorrow, hung her ring
On the wind's finger, was not half so vain.
I sing for you who at the end of summer
Have crowned the year and come together at last.

These nights are kind as the memory of a mother.
The geese track south across the heavy moon.
Your winter will be a triumph of clear decision
And what incredible spring may lie beyond?
O live and love to see your happy children
Deny the sorrow of a burning world.

Though you will have no bells and the winter is coming
I sing your courage, who expect the spring.

October 1942.

North sea

THE evening thickens. Figures like a frieze
Cross the sea's face, their cold unlifted heads
Disdainful of the wind that pulls their hair.
The brown light lies across the harbour wall.

And eastward looking, eastward wondering
I meet the eyes of Heine's ghost, who saw
His failure in the grey forsaken waves
At Rulenstein one autumn. And between
Rises the shape in more than memory
Of Düsseldorf, the ringing, river-enfolding
City that brought such sorrow on us both.

October 1942.

Four postures of death

I

DEATH AND THE MAIDEN

HE said 'Dance for me,' and he said,
'You are too beautiful for the wind
To pick at, or the sun to burn.' He said,
'I'm a poor tattered thing, but not unkind
To the sad dancer and the dancing dead.'

So I smiled and a slow measure
Mastered my feet and I was happy then.
He said, 'My people are gentle as lilies
And in my house there are no men
To wring your young heart with a foolish pleasure.'

Because my boy had crossed me in a strange bed
I danced for him and was not afraid.
He said, 'You are too beautiful for any man
To finger; you shall stay a maid
For ever in my kingdom and be comforted.'

104

He said, 'You shall be my daughter and your feet move
In finer dances, maiden; and the hollow
Halls of my house shall flourish with your singing.'
He beckoned and I knew that I must follow
Into the kingdom of no love.

II

DEATH AND THE LOVERS

The Lover.   The briars fumble with the moon;
Far have I come, O far away
And heartsick sore, my own sweeting.

The Woman.   I stand before the ordered prison room.
I can give you no lover's greeting.

The Lover.   Wind cracks the clouds, so has my face cracked open
With longing all this while, my cold face turning
Hopelessly to you, like a hound's blind muzzle
Turned to the moon.

The Woman.   O you bring in a sickly moon
And you bring in the rain:
I will not open, my true love is gone,
You are his ghost. O never come again.

The Lover.   My feet are bleeding, you called me and your face
Called me a daylong dreary journeying.

The Woman.   Get back, get back into your likely place.
The time is past for all this havering.

The Lover.   I am a poor boy, pity
A poor boy on the roads, after your love.

The Woman.   It is too late: seek out a storied city
To house your silliness. Oh, my lost love . . .

Death.   Is here behind you. Get you in
Out of that muscular salacious wind.
Lie down with me: I have an art
To comfort you and still your restless mind.

The Woman.   I'll close the window; and God send
We are damned easily . . .

Death.	Lie down with me, be gentle: at the end Of time, God's quiet hands will kill your fantasy.
The Lover.	And strangle me, God's horny fingers, huge Fingers of broken cloud, great creaking hands That so beset me; briar-nails tear free My soul into your wisdom, ravish me Since she will not . . .
The Woman.	I am afraid, your hands are strong and cold. Are you my enemy, or my forsaken lover?
Death.	Lie soft, lie still. I am sleep's cruel brother.

III

DEATH AND THE LADY

O quietly I wait by the window and my frayed fine hand
Rests in the autumn sunlight.
                                      Quietly
The garden trees shake down their crown of leaves.
I have no fear because I have no lover.

I was never acquisitive, never would bind
Any man for myself: so from this brown and golden
Season of loneliness let him call me softly—
Expecting my compliance, not my welcome.

It may be an hour's play, this waiting for the word—
He will speak softly, for they all spoke softly—
Or I may fill an autumn with contrition
And waiting for the arm across my shoulders.

Yet he must use no lover's talk to me.
Nor shall his hand be ringed, even with sapphires.
He need not dance, for I have danced with others.
O let him come as bare and white as winter.

The wind comes and goes. The leaves and clouds
Fall through the branches. In a dream
Or perhaps a picture, quite without surprise
I turn to meet the question in his eyes.

DEATH AND THE PLOWMAN

The Rider.   O don't, don't ever ask me for alms:
The winter way I'm riding. Beggar, shun
My jingling bonebag equipage, beware
My horse's lifted hoof, the sinewed whip.
I am the man started a long time since
To drive into the famous land some call
Posterity, some famine, some the valley
Of bones, valley of bones, valley of dry
Bones where a critical mind is always searching
The poor dried marrow for a drop of truth.
Better for you to ask no alms, my friend.

The Plowman.   It's only the wind holds my poor bones together,
So take me with you to that famous land.
There I might wither, as I'm told some do,
Out of my rags and boast at last
The integrated skeleton of truth.

The Rider.   The wind creeps sharper there, my hopeful friend,
Than you imagine. There the crooked trees
Bend like old fingers; and at Hallowmass
The Lord calls erring bones to dance a figure.

The Plowman.   What figure, friend? Why should I fear that dancing?

The Rider.   No man may reasonably dance
That figure, friend. One saw it, one Ezekiel
Was only spared to tell of it. That valley
Is no man's proper goal, but some must seek it.

The Plowman.   I might get clothing there. A skeleton
Cannot go naked.

The Rider.   Naked as the sky
And lonely as the elements, the man
Who knows that land. The drypoint artist there
Scrabbles among the wreckage; poets follow
The hard crevasses, silly as starved gulls
That scream behind the plow. Don't stop me, friend,
Unless you are of those, and your fool's pride
Would lure you to that land. . . .

107

The Plowman.	I will go with you. Better plow-following, the searching wind About my bones than this nonentity.
The Rider.	Then get you up beside me, gull-brained fool.
Both.	We're driving to the famous land some call Posterity, some famine, some the valley Of bones, valley of bones, valley of dry Bones where there is no heat nor hope nor dwelling: But cold security, the one and only Right of a workless man without a home.

from August 1941.

William Byrd

I have come very far, Lord. In my time
Men's mouths have been shut up, the gabble and whine
Of shot has drowned the singing. You will pardon
My praise that rises only from a book—
(How long shall that book be hidden
Under a scarecrow gown, under evil writings?)
And you will pardon the tricks, the secret rooms,
The boarded windows, your house again a stall.
These things have made my house of praise more holy.
And so I try to remember how it was
When lovers sang like finches and the Word
Was music.
          Lord, I am no coward,
But an old man remembering the candle-flames
Reflected in the scroll-work, frozen trees
Praying for Advent, the willow cut at Easter.
The quires are dumb. My spirit sings in silence.
You will appoint the day of my arising.

November 1942.

Moonlight night on the port

SOME were unlucky. Blown a mile to shoreward
Their crossed hands lie among the bitter marsh-grass.

Link arms and sing. The moon sails out
Spreading distraction on the faces, drawing
The useful hands to birdclaws. . . .
                                        If a ring
Flashes, what matter? Other hands are ringless.
We'll never go home to-night, never to-night.

And some shall be pulled down, revolving sickly
On the tide's whim, their bare feet scraping sand.

The moon is out, my lady; lady of different
Voices and gestures, with the same cold eyes.
The buoy swings ringing. Under the curved seawall
My hands reveal your soundings all the same.

Some were more gallant, dragged across the seabed
In iron cages, coughing out their lungs.

Singing in bars, running before the seven
Set winds of the heart; bearing our weakness bravely
Through all the frigid seasons, we have weighed
The chances against us, and refuse no kisses—
Even the tide's kiss on this dog-toothed shore.

For some are lucky, leaving their curved faces
Propped in the moonlight while their bodies drown.

Actaeon's lament

I have beaten the drum and danced. I have seen
Incredible faces peering through the green
Leaves of the sycamore, yet did not lack
Company while the hounds were at my back.

Now hounds cry in my bones as once they cried—
Their eyes turned wise and savage—when I died.
For I was torn to shreds as well you know,
And in my mouth the blue-tongued lichens grow.

Never a girl—it was the greyhound grace
And rhythms of her limbs, that questing face—
Has torn my heart or laid me down so low
Among the fern as she has laid me now.

Jays flirt and haver in the early year.
Heavy upon my unforgetful ear
The hunter's tread resounds, and far away
My crowned hounds celebrate Diana's day.

November 1942.

110

An early death

THIS is the day his death will be remembered
By all who weep:
This the day his grief will be remembered
By all who grieve.
The winds run down the ice-begotten valleys
Bringing the scent of spring, the healing rain.
But the healing hands lie folded like dead birds:
Their stillness is our comfort who have seen him.

But for the mother what can I find of comfort?
She who wrought glory out of bone and planted
The delicate tree of nerves whose foliage
Responded freely to the loving wind?
Her grief is walking through a harried country
Whose trees, all fanged with savage thorns, are bearing
Her boy's pale body worried on the thorns.

Poem from the north

AS I passed under the statue of Mr. Gladstone
The snow came back, dancing down slantwise, whipping
That righteous face with all the old sky's scorn.
And round the corner, in the rubble, strode
Doorways like megaliths of fallen houses
Yet even here, the echo of a horn
Winds through the clutter of chimneys, as the hunter
Runs on the cruel ridge of winter.

The fowl are not taken, the roe not slung
Across hunched shoulders; nor at the steel-grey hour
Of nightfall do the geese rise yelping from the pond.
Here, though, the quarry is life, the kill a token
Of birth to the coughing loiterer under the lamp,
To the lover rising to wash the blood from his hand.

For even statues cannot stand at gaze
Forever, and the times are running.
Winter, the hunter's season, will not pity
The people afraid to be born who crowd the streets
Or those afraid of death who crouch in bed
Behind the darkened windows of this city.
I hear the hunter's horn, the long halloo,
The cold wind beating at a stone-dead statue.

The grail

THE great cup tumbled, ringing like a bell
Thrown down upon the lion-guarded stair
When the cloud took Him; and its iron voice
Challenged the King's dead majesty to fear.

Rise up, Arthur. Galahad grail-seeker
Wails with the pale identical queens on the river.
The sculptured lion raises a clumsy paw:
Bors has lain down beneath the stones of law.

Lie uneasy, Guenever. Lancelot sword-lover
Burnt like a blade will share your bed no more.
Bared his red head, he weeps with shame and sickness—
His pride the sword-bridge to your heart of Gorre.

But the dead girl, the flower-crowned, alone
Walks without fear the bannered streets of heaven;
Lies nightly in the hollow of His hand—
The cradle of your fear her fort and haven.

She alone
Knew from her birth the mystic Avalon.

February 1943.

The Wilderness — *cof.*

I.M. Geoffry Chaucer, George Darley, T.S. Eliot, the other explorers.

(I)

The red rock wilderness
Shall be ~~your~~ dwelling place.

Where the wind saws at the bluffs
And the pebble falls like thunder
~~You~~ I shall watch the clawed sun
Tear the rocks asunder.

The seven-branched cactus
Will never sweat wine:
~~Your~~ My own bleeding feet
Shall furnish the sign. .

The rock says "Endure."
The wind says "Pursue."
The sun says "I will suck your bones
And afterward bury you."

(ii)

Here where the horned skulls mark the limit
Of instinct & intransigeant desire
I beat against the rough-tongued wind
Towards the heart of fire.

So knowing my youth, which was yesterday;

114

The wilderness

I

THE red rock wilderness
Shall be my dwelling-place.

Where the wind saws at the bluffs
And the pebble falls like thunder
I shall watch the clawed sun
Tear the rocks asunder.

The seven-branched cactus
Will never sweat wine:
My own bleeding feet
Shall furnish the sign.

The rock says 'Endure.'
The wind says 'Pursue.'
The sun says 'I will suck your bones
And afterwards bury you.'

II

Here where the horned skulls mark the limit
Of instinct and intransigeant desire
I beat against the rough-tongued wind
Towards the heart of fire.

So knowing my youth, which was yesterday,
And my pride which shall be gone to-morrow,
I turn my face to the sun, remembering gardens
Planted by others—Longinus, Guillaume de Lorris
And all love's gardeners, in an early May.
O sing, small ancient bird, for I am going
Into the sun's garden, the red rock desert
I have dreamt of and desired more than the lilac's promise.
The flowers of the rock shall never fall.

O speak no more of love and death
And speak no word of sorrow:
My anger's eaten up my pride
And both shall die to-morrow.

Knowing I am no lover, but destroyer,
I am content to face the destroying sun.
There shall be no more journeys, nor the anguish
Of meeting and parting, after the last great parting
From the images of dancing and the gardens
Where the brown bird chokes in its song:
Until that last great meeting among mountains
Where the metal bird sings madly from the fire.

O speak no more of ceremony,
Speak no more of fame:
My heart must seek a burning land
To bury its foolish pain.

By the dry river at the desert edge
I regret the speaking rivers I have known;
The sunlight shattered under the dark bridge
And many tongues of rivers in the past.
Rivers and gardens, singing under the willows,
The glowing moon. . . .
                                        And all the poets of summer
Must lament another spirit's passing over.

O never weep for me, my love,
Or seek me in this land:
But light a candle for my luck
And bear it in your hand.

III

In this hard garden where the earth's ribs
Lie bare from her first agony, I seek
The home of the gold bird, the predatory Phoenix.
O louder than the tongue of any river
Call the red flames among the shapes of rock:
And this is my calling. . . .
                                        Though my love must sit
Alone with her candle in a darkened room
Listening to music that is not present or
Turning a flower in her childish hands
And though we were a thousand miles apart . . .
This is my calling, to seek the red rock desert

And speak for all those who have lost the gardens,
Forgotten the singing, yet dare not find the desert—
To sing the song that rises from the fire.
    It is not profitable to remember
How my friends fell, my heroes turned to squalling
Puppets of history; though I would forget
The way of this one's failure, that one's exile—
How the small foreign girl
Grew crazed with her own beauty; how the poet
Talks to the wall in a deserted city;
How others danced until the Tartar wind
Blew in the doors; or sitting alone at midnight
Heard Solomon Eagle beat his drum in the streets:
This is the time to ask their pardon
For any act of coldness in the past.
There is no kind of space can separate us:
No weather, even this cruel sun, can change us;
No dress, though you in shining satin walk
Or you in velvet, while I run in tatters
Against the fiery wind. There is no loss,
Only the need to forget. This is my calling. . . .
    But behind me the rattle of stones underfoot,
Stones from the bare ridge rolling and skidding:
A voice I know, but had consigned to silence,
Another calling: my own words coming back. . . .

'And I would follow after you
Though it were a thousand mile:
Though you crossed the deserts of the world to the kingdom of
    death, my dear,
I would follow after you and stand beside you there.'

IV

Who is this lady, flirting with the wind,
Blown like a tangle of dried flowers through the desert?
This is my lover whom I left
Alone at evening between the candles—
White fingers nailed with flame—in an empty house.
Here we have come to the last ridge, the river
Crossed and the birds of summer left to silence.
And we go forth, we go forth together

With our lank shadows dogging us, scrambling
Across the raw red stones.
                                    There is no parting
From friends, but only from the ways of friendship;
Nor from our lovers, though the forms of love
Change often as the landscape of this journey
To the dark valley where the gold bird burns.
I say, Love is a wilderness and these bones
Proclaim no failure, but the death of youth.
We say, You must be ready for the desert
Even among the orchards starred with blossom,
Even in spring, or at the waking moment
When the man turns to the woman, and both are afraid.
All who would save their life must find the desert—
The lover, the poet, the girl who dreams of Christ,
And the swift runner, crowned with another laurel:
They all must face the sun, the red rock desert,
And see the burning of the metal bird.
Until you have crossed the desert and faced that fire
Love is an evil, a shaking of the hand,
A sick pain draining courage from the heart

We do not know the end, we cannot tell
That valley's shape, nor whether the white fire
Will blind us instantly. . . .
                                    Only we go
Forward, we go forward together, leaving
Nothing except a worn-out way of loving.

V

Flesh is fire, the fire of flesh burns white
Through living limbs: a cold fire in the blood.
We must learn to live without love's food.

We shall see the sky without birds, the wind
Will blow no leaves, will ruffle no new river.
We shall walk in the desert together.
Flesh is fire, frost and fire.
We have turned in time, we shall see
The Phoenix burning under a rich tree.
Flesh is fire.

118

Solomon Eagle's drum shall be filled with sand:
The dancers shall wear out their skilful feet,
The pretty lady be wrapped in a rough sheet.

We go now, but others must follow:
The rivers are drying, the trees are falling,
The red rock wilderness is calling.

And they will find who linger in the garden
The way of time is not a river but
A pilferer who will not ask their pardon.

Flesh is fire, frost and fire:
Flesh is fire in this wilderness of fire
Which is our dwelling.

December 1942–January 1943.

South wind

I stand alone amid the velvet dusk
Where she and I of old did use to meet,
Just at this time upon a Summer eve,
Here on the hill above the nodding wheat.

The wind blows softly from the South;
Ripples among the golden corn.
Oh, where is she that she comes not,
Though I wait from dusk to dawn?

Wind from the South, Summer wind,
Bring her back to me;
Bring her back to my arms again,
Just as she used to be.

She never knew I loved her so,
When on this hill we used to meet,
But now she's gone, and I am left,
Desolate, over the whispering wheat.

Oh, gentle wind from out the South,
Tell me, where is she gone,
That she comes not to meet me here,
Though I wait from dusk to dawn?

July 1934 (aet. 12 years 2 months)

Cathay

A scented dream; a twisted vision quaint;
Another world, of fragile symmetry.
So far away, but yet its pipes squeal faint—
Its tinkling music will not leave my ears.

I cannot help but dream of far Cathay,
And when they ask me how I know these things
I answer not, and sadly turn away—
Though I can hear the fluttering of the wings
Of golden pigeons, and their burbling din,
As they strut, jostling, puffed with jerky pride
Before a dragon-temple in Pekin.

June 1937 (aet. 15)

Meditation of Phlebas the Phoenician

WHICH is the path? There are too many ways;
And all entice my feet—
The palpitating dove-wings of the maze,
Or silence in the street.

What is the goal? Oh, there are many ends
Which pull my soul apart—
The terminus where lines' mad tangle blends,
Or silence in the heart.

Why must I go? I am a corpse long-drowned,
Tricked out in foamy lace:
Spindrift and terror tumble all around
The silence in your face.

January 1939

Richmond Park

STAG-ANTLERED oaks loom by the track;
Huge, fog hanging in their horns, they rear.
Through the crisp swish of bracken we hear
Them belling and roaring afar, but do not look back.

This park has always been misty, uncouth
And bestial, since King Henry ran the deer.
This was a place then of killing, full of fear
When he hunted the stags here in the pride of his youth.

Herne, too, hunts the thickets sere
Homeless and hanged, poor Herne—
The antlered idiot who will learn
No other wisdom but following the deer.

The bracken drips; ghosts of dead deer
Bellow by the unseen stream forlorn.
Winding the coverts of my heart, a horn
Brays and astonishes the heavy air.

1940

Blues song

SNOW ain't falling
Snow ain't falling today.
I met my girl this dirty morning
But she wasn't going my way.

O it's sure freezing
I said, it's freezing to the bone.
I met my girl this afternoon—
She said, 'Why ain't you home?'

It's grey slush on the sidewalks
Grey cold in the sky:
If I meet my girl this evening
I'll just lay down and die.

Blues

MOONLIGHT shining all round the square:
I went after you last night
But you weren't there.

Poolroom was open but I didn't stay:
I went after you this morning
But you'd gone away.

All afternoon I sat by the door
Till someone told me
You wouldn't come home no more.

When they told me you'd got another man
I drank a pint of poison
From a big tin can.

Sun's going down like a roll of drums—
I ain't moving
Until the hearse comes.

Bix blues

BIX was a boy from New Orleans
Yes, he was raised in New Orleans—
And I don't have to tell you what that means.

One day a nigger give him a horn
And he starts to blow that fine new horn:
You ain't heard nothing like it since you were born.

Chorus, repeat after each verse
    Oh he blew all night and he blew all day
    And he blew that horn till he blew his heart away.

Christmas it was and white with frost
Christmas and the groun' was white with frost:
But when he blew that horn, the buds began to burst.

There was a corpse laid out next door
There was an old stiff laid out next door:
But when it heard that horn, it got up and danced on the floor.

When Gabriel up in heaven heard that horn blow
When Mr. Gabriel heard Bix's horn blow
He said 'O my Lord, what d'you know?'

So Bix took his horn and joined a band
He joined a red-hot dixie band,
And there wasn't a better horn in all the land.

He didn't smoke and he didn't play dice,
He never went with girls and he never played dice,
And there wasn't a better horn this side of Paradise.

But pretty soon he got drinking rye
Pretty soon he got full of rye:
Then he got a drag and he wanted to die.

One day he was blowing, he let out a shout
He stopped blowing and gave a shout—
Then he fell to the ground and passed right out.

They put him in bed but he only got worse
He was mighty sick and he kept getting worse
Till he turned up his toes and they sent for the hearse.

At the morgue they tied him in a sack
They tied him up in a two-cent sack,
But he hollered out, 'You give my horn back!'

So they put that horn right by his mouth
They put that horn right up to his mouth
And they buried him six foot down in the earth.

Preacher said, 'He's a sinner, he won't never rise,
No, he'll burn, he won't never rise'.
But all them niggers was crying out their eyes.

But 'A man like that' his mammy said
'A man like that', his mammy said,
'A man like that won't never stay dead'.

'Oh he blew his guts and his heart away
He blew his lovely heart away—
But I guess he'll be blowing on Judgement Day!'

February 2nd 1941

Letter to M.C., 31.vii.41

NOW that, my dearest, it is darkening and
The small rain enters my valley, I think of others
Who would not be amazed at war; who held
Their stinted plot of mind with awkward courage
Against the logic of historians
And women's quick contempt. And were not forgotten.

Now that the scent of stocks invades my windows
I think of gun-torn Germany under Napoleon's
Calipers cut, under his wheeltracks furrowed:
And Goethe working by his quiet candle
Undaunted by the soldiery, content
To rule the steadfast empire of the heart.

Or is Jas du Bouffan, and the painter
Strains nature's image through his mind's clear prism;
While in the North, one bitter myth
Grapples another, sowing tears like teeth.
But when their myths are broken, his remain—
Victory, a mountain green and big with peace.

These were the strong, though some could not escape:
Stendhal among the snow and the spiked canon
Of eighteen twelve, would shave that surgeon's face
Without respect for the cold, the frozen blood.
And Goya fought an inner war, vomiting
His nightmares on to paper for a warning.

Tonight I'm thinking of these and of you, my dearest;
Sheltered but not secure in my country pleasures.
We must create our peace, our war is private.
For while you face the canvas and my hand
Walks on the paper, we can take
No rest nor comfort, but must learn their courage.

For Milein, 1.xii.41

TALK stopped, and the five-fingered hand of sense
Crouched like a creature. Your amazing eyes
Swung inward suddenly, pulling me down
Among the debris of my broken gestures.
And there were lives perversely otherwise
Than ours, yet like; and possible
Solutions to the fearsome riddle
That ravished my mind's country. There was Chartres
Reeling with insult; my own vanity
Of clockwork bird and painted loneliness
Rubble upon that place, rabble upon
The guarded stairs of your mind's secret place.
And there were pictured rivers unexplored
By us; and unmapped forests we could tame
With my hard hand and your bright eyes to guide it.

126

There were the foundling hours now wandering
Homeless and eager for our saving friendship.
There was a lake, Mozart beside a lake
Plucking the bitter-fruited orange Fame;
Long ways of hopeful windows; the old year
Stretching its straitjacket of ice and crying
For us to rescue summer. All these images
Lay in that place.
                              Words fell between the picture
And its projection, as your face changed quickly.
Rilke a moment wandered between our eyes
Gazing in each, seeing in separation
A central unity: the whitestone angel standing
Between us irrefutably, teaching our world
Humility and peace. Our peace, our poem.

Premature poem for Milein

Darkness at eight, the day's most courteous
Agreement with my mood, gives way to sun.
Then, entering the southward gallery hung
With our new ancestors, we laugh and run.
Friendly in sheer surprise, time shelters us.

The wind slides on the river; grasses raise
Their heads to share our vision. In the street
Traffic forgets to threaten; and we meet
No dead ironic faces, spade-shaped feet
As once companioned our uncertain days.

What has the human tide, the long night done?
I dare not thank the moon's or body's phase:
Content to join with the illustrious
Line of the loved, the lucky, the complete.

15–16th December 1941.

Mr. U Saw Blues

U Saw he done right
I say, Mr. U Saw he done right
He tried to save his country from the British Imperialist Blight.

Mr. U Saw he went to the Japs
Mr. U Saw Prime Minister of Burma said to the Japs:
'You come on in; these British are just a crowd of saps'.

But the British government got U Saw in Hawaii
The British government caught U Saw in Hawaii.
The British government said, 'We're sure going to make you groan
   and sigh'.

So they shut U Saw up in jail house
They shut U Saw up in the dirty jail house.
They said, 'You ain't minister no more, you damn louse'.

They shut U Saw up in the British Government jail
They shut U Saw up in the British Government jail:
And there won't be no visitors, and there won't be no bail.

They shut U saw up with nobody to hear his moans
They shut him away from telegraphs and phones;
And bye and bye they started to beat the hide off his bones.

Now this is the last we'll hear of U Saw
I'm saying, we won't never hear no more about U Saw—
Because he stood by his country, and that's against British Imperial
   Law.

A Translation of Carmen XI by Catullus*

O friends, my stedfast fellow-travellers—
Whether I seek the coasts of India
Pounded by hollow seas; Hyrcania
Or soft Arabia seek; or should I wander
Among the swift steppe-archers, Parthians and Saga;
Whether I'm crossing the red fields of Egypt
Dyed by the seven-headed Nile;
Walking the Alps after great Caesar's monuments;
Crossing the Gallic Rhine; still my companions
Among the savage tribes at the world's end—
O friends who'd go these ways with me, whatever
Danger or profit the high gods may send us,
Take these words to my girl, these few hard words:
'Be happy with the men you do not love,
Yet suck them dry, three hundred in a night.
And never look to me for love again—
My love's like any flower of the fallow
Cut down and wasted by the passing plow.'

May 1942

---

* 'I enclose also my own inept effort to translate Catullus. You may wonder Why Catullus? and I can only say that there is a volume of him in the local library with crib opposite. I have also read, in the same book, a fine late Latin poem (almost mediaeval) called *Pervigilium Veneris*, which has the refrain 'cras amet qui nunquam amavit, quique amavit cras amet' [he shall love tomorrow who has never loved, and he who has loved shall love tomorrow] which is as pleasant a thought as could occur to anyone.' (Letter from Keyes in Dunbar to John Heath Stubbs, May 24th 1942.)

Cold comfort for Mr. Meyer*

Poète et non honnête homme (Pascal)

So he could say, climbing his twisted scaffold
Above the pit of intellectual pride.
Let any man strike a hard fist against us,
We echo dully. There is nothing inside.

Our ancestors all turned to drugs and drink;
Our children will be acrobats or fools.
In twenty years the only thing we've learnt
Is how to lose the game and keep the rules.

We have no principles but strong opinions.
We are not honest and we do not care.
Only in verses or the cricket field
We move with some assurance. Only there.

June 1942

---

*Another typescript of this poem is entitled *Birthday Poem for Michael Meyer*.

APPENDIX 2

Sidney Keyes as a Soldier

by James Lucas

Sidney Keyes served with me in 14 Platoon, C Company, 1st Battalion the Queen's Own Royal West Kent Regiment; he as the platoon commander and I as a private soldier.

We met in January or February 1943, when the battalion was stationed at Hawick, Roxburghshire, preparing for overseas service as part of the 4th British Infantry Division. The deadness of a Scottish Sabbath caused Sunday to be considered as a work day in the battalion and Thursday was our day of rest. One Thursday morning 14 Platoon was still abed when Keyes entered the barrack room. His question showed that he had not been advised of the substitution of the Sabbath for he asked why we were not up and ready for first parade. One of my comrades—Box, I think—sleeping in the cot opposite mine asked who the hell he was and was told the new Platoon commander. Box then asked whether the officer could read and advised him to go across to the ablution hut and read Standing Orders. A few minutes later Keyes returned and gently apologized for having disturbed us.

I should explain that the great mass of 1st Battalion were Cockneys and most were regular soldiers with years of experience of fighting in the colonies and, more recently, in France during 1940. Such men had seen officers come and go and could sum up their superiors very quickly. They summed Keyes up in a flash as being 'dead cush'—not a rigid disciplinarian. In truth, Keyes was not a strutting, martial man of war and when he mounted guard as Orderly Officer he drew a mob of spectators who came to see what sartorial eccentricity he would display. On one occasion he wore his web anklets upside down. His first batman—Slattery, I think—was a real lout who claimed that he drank the officer's whisky. Foster, his second batman, was a gentler person more akin to Keyes' own nature.

On the troop ship that took us to Africa, Keyes lectured us on a variety of subjects. It is very easy to get bored on a ten-day cruise when the only form of entertainment is housey-housey or cards. His lectures were on poetry, on Gibraltar—which we passed one night—and as soon as our destination was known (Algiers), on French North Africa. From the brick works at Maison Carrée where we were first billeted, Keyes took us on educational trips to nearby Roman ruins. He was a keen ornithologist and also showed us a distant mountain mass shining in the sun—the Atlas mountains. He knew about the soil, the plants, the vegetation and he also spoke French. His lecturing style was not easy for he talked as if we were his intellectual peers—which we were not and much of which he said went over our heads, but his approach was a change from the standard, 'Sit up straight at the back there; we're having a talk today on the Bren gun.'

We sailed from Algiers to Bone and disembarked in the middle of a particularly violent air raid. As I was Keyes' runner and, therefore, had to stay close to him I was able to observe his coolness during the bombing. Not until his men were safe did he himself take cover. En route to the front, probably about the time we reached Beja, he left us to go on a mine course, identifying the various types and rendering them safe. By the time we had reached the Oued Zarga hills he had rejoined the platoon. The battalion was stretched out along the crest of the Oued Zarga ridge—on the reverse slope in daylight, on the forward slope by night—with C Company forming the right flank. Keyes' platoon formed the left flank of the Company touching B Company's right flank. Oued Zarga was a quiet sector although there had been a bitter battle for the heights and the dead had not all been buried. It was on Oued Zarga that I heard one night a piper of the Argylls playing a lament for the fallen—a most emotional experience.

Keyes had an unusual habit for a front-line infantryman. He lined his slit trench with an American Army issue blanket so that no pieces of loose soil fell upon him while he sat in it or slept in it. So far as I remember he fixed the blanket into position with metal tent pegs or meat skewers. He wrote some poetry while we were on Oued Zarga and also did some bird watching although there were few in the area. He was also very interested in the types of beetles that infested the body of a dead, wolf-like dog that lay unburied near our platoon positions.

The crest of Oued Zarga was covered in a sort of broom-like plant having heavily scented, yellow flowers. I was on guard, one day, in an observation trench on the crest, when Keyes came up the slope, lay down and showed me the ground over which he, Corporal Gibson and I were to patrol that night. During that reconnaissance patrol I suddenly heard our officer speaking German, berating someone for sleeping on duty. When Gibson and I closed up, Keyes told us that the figure, reclining in a very relaxed position on a rock, was dead. There was no smell of corruption, nor could we make out, by starlight, any visible wounds. Until that time I had not known that Keyes spoke German.

As I have already said, most of the battalion were Cockneys and included some loud-mouthed types of the 'let me get at the Jerry' variety. Keyes took two such out on patrol. Halfway through the night he told them that he was going off by himself to reconnoitre and that they were to stay in position for they were now miles behind the German lines. You can well imagine the state of their nerves when the officer came back and rejoined them.

On 28th April we launched a two-Company attack upon ground to the north of Peter's Corner, on the road to Tunis. C Company had as its objective Point 133. We crossed the start line at 7.30 p.m. under a heavy barrage. As Keyes' runner my position was to be by his side. We walked together through the gloom of the brief twilight, the smoke of the explosions and the dust. He pointed at something on the ground and told me that it was the German sign marking a mine field. We were, therefore, crossing one. In a conversational tone he remarked that there would be S mines sown in the area and that these exploded twice. One minor explosion to propel an inner casing into the air; the second explosion ripped that casing, propelling 360 ballbearings at waist height. Keyes told me that should there be an explosion under my foot I should keep it in position and thus prevent the case from springing up. The second explosion, he told me, would blow my foot off, but that it was better for me to lose a foot than for the platoon to suffer casualties from the explosion.

A little farther on Keyes moved to the right to speak to Sergeant Bourne and I was about to follow him when I saw in front of me an MG 34 on a tripod. Behind it was a trench filled with Germans, some of whom I shot. Corporal Rudling, seeing me in action, came and together we wiped out the other Germans in the trench. When I caught up with Keyes and the rest of the platoon our line was halted and he was arranging for prisoners to be sent back to the battalion positions. The Company was halted at the bottom of a short slope covered with wheat. Our objective was the crest of the hill. Keyes ordered us to fix bayonets and we advanced up the slope. On the crest the Company formed hollow square with 14 Platoon taking up position as the left side. The time would then have been about 9 in the evening.

Orders were given for us to consolidate on the position. This meant to dig trenches and to prepare ourselves for a German counter-attack. We could not dig very deeply into the soil of Point 133 for there were large rocks at a depth of about two feet and we had only our entrenching tools. We, therefore, made scrape holes and lay in them.

At about 2 in the morning, so far as I could judge, some of 14 Platoon were ordered to go out on patrol. There were about nine men selected. I was told to stay behind with Sergeant Bourne and the rest of the Platoon. With the patrol gone there was a gap in the square and it had to be closed. The Company Commander reorganized our positions. Those of us from 14 Platoon were then moved to form the bottom edge of the square. We lay in the wet wheat waiting for dawn and the German counter-attack.

Just after first light, paratroops from (I think) No. 2 Company, 1st battalion, 5th Para Regiment—by that time renamed as the Hermann Goering Jaeger battalion—attacked and overran us. The Company Commander was shot through the stomach, others were killed and many wounded. The rest of us were taken prisoner. From what I have learned since that time Keyes' patrol, which had the task of 'sweeping' the Company front, was attacked by the German paratroops moving forward to assault the Company square. Keyes and another man— Smith or Williams 09—were last seen standing shoulder-to-shoulder firing Tommy guns at the oncoming Germans. The rest of the patrol, on Keyes' order, tried to get back into the Company square. It is believed that Keyes and the other man fell in action at that time and in that place. That the bodies were found so far from our Company position on the crest of Point 133 accounts, perhaps, for Colonel Haycraft's theory that both had been wounded, taken from the scene of the action and had died while prisoners. I think that this is unlikely because troops in a counter-attack situation do not bother to remove the wounded from the field—they have more urgent priorities. Nor did the German officers who interrogated me mention that they had taken prisoner one of our officers. It would have been a standard interrogation ploy—'We have one of your officers, Lt. Keyes, and he has told us that . . .' The German officers did not mention the capture of a British officer.

When we were taken prisoner we had only one officer still standing. Keyes was with his patrol, the Company Commander was wounded, the 2 i/c was one of the LOB's (left out of battle) and the surviving Lieutenant took down his 'pip' to avoid being taken away from us.

During my Army service I had a number of Platoon commanders. Keyes was the best of them. His was the quiet, determined, non-blustering type of leadership. His manners were impeccable and he did not talk down to us, nor was he condescending towards us—so many officers were. He was a gallant, Christian gentleman who sacrificed himself for the men under his command.

NOTES

Keyes invariably destroyed the rough drafts of his poems, after he had completed them to his satisfaction. His MSS., written in a large, clear hand, therefore present few textual problems. But while a poem was in progress he often discussed the details and problems of it with his friends, and it seemed worth while to gather our reminiscences while they are still vivid. I have also included relevant extracts from his diary and letters; and have attempted to elucidate references to historical and mythological personages where an ignorance of these might obscure the significance of the poem.

Nocturne for Four Voices. Page 4
  'This is a dream-poem . . . in a way an attempt at abstract (i.e. "musical") poetry, a modification of the symphonic technique.'

(Keyes' footnote.)

Shall the Dead Return? Page 9
  Keyes destroyed the MS. of this poem in displeasure, and the only extant copy ends with the lines:
            Now I can answer Mr. Eliot's question.
            They don't want to return but they must.
This conclusion is so obviously makeshift that I felt justified in printing the body of the poem as a fragment.

Remember your Lovers. Page 14
  This poem was written in an examination room, after Keyes had finished his paper. Later, he reacted against what he called its 'lush sentimentality,' and excluded it from *The Iron Laurel*, together with *Greenwich Observatory* and *Cervières*. The first two poems were only inserted into *The Cruel Solstice* as an afterthought, after the rest of the book had been accepted for publication. *Greenwich Observatory* was likewise written in an examination room after Keyes had finished a paper for his scholarship at Queen's.

Sour Land. Page 15
  Keyes once said that he thought the line
            So to his perch appropriate with owls
the best single line he had written, because the epithet 'appropriate' answered to Yeats' demand for 'the intellectually surprising word which is also the correct word.' This was, of course, before he had written most of his best work.

William Yeats in Limbo. Page 17

'William Yeats said to Dorothy Wellesley that after death the soul spends some twenty years in a kind of limbo, like the state between sleeping and waking. He also said, at another time: 'Those who have seen the bodies of spirits, cannot bear the sight of human flesh.' Pallas and Adonis symbolizes the Yeats-Wellesley relationship.' (Keyes' footnote.)

Keyes remarked that, in their letters. Yeats always seemed to write as the woman and Dorothy Wellesley as the man.

Paul Klee. Page 22

'I enclose two of mine: the short one arose out of my visit to the Klee exhibition while in London. You may miss the point if you don't know Klee, but anyway it is quite slight.' (S. K., in a letter to John Heath Stubbs, 8th April 1941.)

Gilles de Retz Page 24

Keyes' main source of information about this figure was Charles Williams' *Witchcraft*, supplemented by Margaret Murray's *The God of the Witches*. He interpreted de Retz as a noble and courageous figure, and said: 'He was the sort of man on whose mind perversion would leave a deep wound.' Subsequently, he planned to arrange a series of elegies on the model of Rilke's, with pain as one of its central themes, including this poem, *A Garland for John Clare, Schiller Dying, The Buzzard, Sour Land, Wantage Downs* (an inferior and unpublished fragment), and another poem, never written, which was to begin with a reference to Walt Whitman's 'There was a boy went forth . . .'

> The incarnation of mortal pride,
> The yearning of immortals for the flesh . . .

i.e. Joan of Arc, with whom de Retz had been associated many years before. The yearning of immortals for the flesh, which Keyes first found in Rilke, seemed to him a theme of the greatest importance.

The Anti-Symbolist. Page 27

Keyes' room at Queen's looked out over the church and graveyard of St. Peter's in the East. From his window he saw the old woman and her dog, whom she called and then laughed loudly and unaccountably. The incident seemed to him as if it should have some significance which it had not—that is the theme of the poem. Hy Brasil is a mythical underwater island in Irish folk-lore.

Plowman. Page 28

Here, for the first time, Keyes uses the workless plowman as a symbol for the poet. The plowman is an early nineteenth-century figure, who has lost his livelihood by enclosures.

Neutrality. Page 29

'*Neutrality* is one of the poems for which I have—I can't tell why—genuine affection. It came so suddenly and so easily, without any previous consideration, that it is remarkable how finished it is, though it hasn't any deep feeling in it.' (S. K., in a letter to J. H. S., 8th August 1941.) Keyes thought for a while of altering the title to *New England*, '40.

Extracts from 'A Journey through Limbo.' Page 32

Keyes intended this as a long narrative poem, but never completed it. The scene is set in Central Europe.

William Wordsworth. Page 35

Suggested by the impressive death-mask which forms the frontispiece to Herbert Read's *Wordsworth*. Keyes said: 'Isn't that fine! *That* is everything which I mean by

Wordsworth,' and then added, 'Even so, it is, in a way, a sheep-like old face.' This poem and *Pheasant* were intended to form part of a sequence of sonnets with *All Souls* (see below).

The Glass Tower in Galway. Page 36

Based on the story of the Tuatha de Danaaen and the Fomors. The last section of the poem was written first, as a lament for Imperial Rome (he had just been reading Robert Graves' *I Claudius*). This and *A Letter from Tartary* were written while he was recovering from a painful operation on his nose, which he thought might account for the predominance of images of pain in the two poems.

All Souls. Page 41

Keyes planned a sequence of sonnets in imitation of Rilke's *Sonnets to Orpheus*. Besides this set of poems, it was to include several dedicated to mighty figures from the past who had influenced him—Wordsworth, El Greco, Rilke and Yeats. Only the first of these was ever written. There were also to be sonnets about things seen, e.g. *Pheasant*. He abandoned the plan because he found the sonnet form cramping, 'as if I had shut myself up in a number of little boxes.' J. H. S. observes that he made the mistake of taking Rilke's very free, advanced and individual treatment of the sonnet form as his model, without understanding the dynamics of the orthodox sonnet. These poems have in reality no characteristic of the sonnet, except that they are limited to fourteen lines. Rilke's *Sonnets to Orpheus*, although very free, never abandon the basic sonnet structure.

'The drinking menhir . . .' alludes to a Breton folk-tale. Two men discover that on one night of the year the menhirs (a type of monolith) leave their places and go down to the river to drink. They plan to steal the treasures buried underneath the menhirs, but one of the thieves, delaying too long, is crushed by the returning menhir as a punishment for his avarice.

Holstenwall. Page 47

This poem refers to the film *The Cabinet of Dr. Caligari*, in one scene of which a hypnotized man is passed off as a ventriloquist's doll.

Against a Second Coming. Page 49

The opening section, *Spring Night*, was written in February 1941, long before the rest of the poem and without any thought of a sequel. The germ of the remainder was two lines which Keyes had jotted down in his Tonbridge days without any intended significance:

> . . . and when you are dead,
> The iron acanthus shall crown your head.

The following note on the sequence appears among Keyes' papers: 'A commentary on this allusive poem may be useful, though any such must necessarily be interpretive rather than explanatory. I conceive it rather as a series of symbolic devices than as a sequence of thought or of narrative; and the main themes are roughly as follows:

'I. *Spring Night*. An introduction. The poet, or *conscious* part of the individual, attempts to prevent the return of (*a*) the dead ("another people") and finally (*b*) the lover. This latter may be considered as Christ, who has been so long away; or, less particularly, as the principle of love itself. He tries to prevent its coming because he does not understand it, and is afraid that, after its long absence, it will return in a terrible form.

'II. *The Walking Woman*. She symbolizes the unreasoning or *sub-conscious* part of the individual, who wishes the return of the lover in spite of the denial of the conscious part. She sees the lover as entirely to be wished for, as an idealized version of her own man who is dead. Being eternal, he cannot be unfaithful.

137

'III. *The Lover*. The lover returns; but it is as the poet thought. The house of hate has been so long closed against him, that he comes as a monster to take it. He is now the accuser also.

'IV. *The Witness*. The poet witnesses before the accuser that he did his best to prevent the return; "it was the woman's blame." He realizes that he must be condemned, but demands that the accuser shall recognize that he has been conquered only by guile, not by his own weakness.

'V. *The Dead Man's Crown*. The poet is inevitably condemned; but his strength is acknowledged and his skull is crowned. Like Nisus, who was betrayed by the woman Sylla to the besieger Minos; or like Constantine, who was almost betrayed to Attila by Honoria, he is condemned but not defeated. Nisus was turned by the gods into an eagle, traditional symbol of the artist and of immortality; and Sylla into a goldfinch. He does not lie among the common dead, but triumphs even in death over his accuser and besieger, the invincible lover.'

The Island City. Page 55
'Yeats' gold song-bird.' This symbol, taken from Yeats' two Byzantium poems, recurs frequently throughout Keyes' later work.

Schiller Dying. Page 55
Keyes began this with the intention of composing a poem about Poe, and only altered his purpose after he had put the opening line on paper. He had been reading a good deal of Schiller, whom he declared he considered superior to Goethe (an unorthodox opinion—but he had never read *Faust!*). He particularly admired the Wallenstein cycle of dramas, which he likened to a modern epic. The poem abounds with references to Schiller's work, e.g.: a poem about Pegasus bridled (lines 4–7); *Wallenstein* ('born under Saturn'); *The Cranes of Ibycus* ('Joy is waylaid and slain . . . The cranes are crying . . .'); and throughout, of course, to the *Ode to Joy*, in which the word 'joy' is substituted for 'freedom'.

Little Drawda. Page 58
Little Drawda is a Jacobean cottage standing in its own garden in the grounds of Queen's College, and supposed to be haunted. People passing at night down the lane that leads to the garden from the back quadrangle said that they felt a sudden and unaccountable chill at a certain spot. Keyes claimed to have experienced this.

The Foreign Gate. Page 66
Keyes began writing this at great pressure after he had already prepared the rest of *The Iron Laurel* for publication. He would have liked to call it *Ruins and Visions*, if a set of poems under that title had not recently been published. The piece is dominated by Rilke ('a pale unlearned poet'), but was influenced towards its close by a poem of J. H. S. based on Chaucer's *House of Fame*. Few of the many literary references have been traced to their ultimate source; Donne had his portrait 'limned in grave-clothes,' and the fine image towards the close:

> . . . embracing bravely the white limbs,
> Engulfed in the long shining hair . . .

was based on Epstein's statue 'Jacob and the Angel,' which Keyes had seen when it was exhibited in London. The lines:

> Were I to cry, who in that proud hierarchy
> Of the illustrious would pity me?

are a direct translation of the first line and a half of Rilke's *Duino Elegies*.

138

Simon Magus. Page 76

In Charles Williams' *The Descent of the Dove*, Keyes found the story that Simon Magus used to be accompanied by a virgin, his disciple, with whom he used to sleep— but not sexually.

Lament for Harpsichord. Page 78

Suggested by Couperin's *Les Vergiers Fleuris*.

The Uncreated Images. Page 86

An apocalyptic passage on the same theme appears in Keyes' diary: "Who are they, and what would they say if they could speak, the tall figures with stony faces and holes for eyes, who stand by the window these summer nights? Why have I never seen them before? Because one can only become entirely sensitive by emptying the mind: then it can be filled by all kinds of uncreated archetypal images.'

The Gardener. Page 92

Keyes originally called this *Poet and Muse*, basing it on the painting of that name by Rousseau Douanier.

The Kestrels. Page 95

'There is very much more struggle for me in love . . . It is a kind of battle as well as a fulfilment; rather like, at times, the moment of drowning when one is said to *want* to go under. My own quotation on the subject would be from Louis MacNeice:

'As men in springtime seek their death in women.'

I've tried to convey it in my own poem, *The Kestrels:* the feeling of two bodies violently colliding and swinging apart, high up in the air. I find it wildly exhilarating . . .' (S. K., in a letter to Renée-Jane Scott, 30th August 1942.)

Dido's Lament for Aeneas. Page 96

'I am extremely ungrateful and proud and self-willed, as you say; life with me would be very difficult, even for you; I am probably rather less weak than you think, but also rather more deliberately destructive; in some ways I'm as blind as a wall, and at some times quite crazy . . .' (S. K., in a letter to R. J. S., 30th August 1942.)

Rome Remember. Page 97

'I have begun to write a poem which is still another lament—for Rome and Carthage, for poetry and learning, for the innocent seasons and for us, who must be anarchists because the age is against us.' (S. K., in a letter to R. J. S., 26th July 1942.)

But the next day he wrote to the same correspondent: 'My poem about Rome and Carthage became horrible at the end, so I will not send it. It is certainly a "goblin" kind of thing.'

The title of the piece is the burden of a poem by Lydgate.

The Expected Guest. Page 102

The Guest is the dying god, Christ and Adonis. Veronica, according to the legend, wiped Christ's face as He was going to the Crucifixion, and her handkerchief miraculously bore the imprint of His features.

Epithalamium. Page 103

Lieutenant Brian Scott, for whose marriage this was written, died in the same battle as Sidney Keyes.

Four Postures of Death. Page 104

These poems were written separately, not being conceived as a sequence until later. Keyes also began a poem on *Death and the Emperor*, which was never finished, and of which no trace remains.

Death and the Maiden was suggested by the slow movement of Schubert's quartet which bears the same name.

Death and the Lovers was originally called *Dialogue at a Window*. In the Countess Cesaresco's *Essays in the Study of Folk-Songs*, there is an account of the song known as *Fensterlied*, in which a woman sings to her baby a lullaby the words of which warn her lover outside that her husband is at home. The speeches given to Death were originally spoken by the Husband, and were only altered so that the poem might fit into the sequence. The earlier version ended.

> HUSBAND   Lie soft, lie still. We will create another.

which was intended to illustrate Keyes' theory that sex, regarded as the instrument of reproduction, was only an instrument for creating more sex. By making the alteration, as J. H. S. observes, he seems rather to have obscured the issue of the poem and weakened the ending.

Death and the Lady was suggested by a broadsheet dialogue of the same title in Bell's *Ballads and Songs of the Peasantry of England*.

Death and the Plowman was originally entitled *Death and the Beggar*.

Moonlight Night on the Port. Page 109

A variation on this mood occurs as a late entry in Keyes' diary: 'Latitude of Bordeaux, 19. iii. 43. The sea doesn't impress or obsess me very much; it is just a lot of water. I only wonder why so much of this planet is covered with the stuff we call Water. Perhaps we are deceived, and the important life of the world goes on under the water? But I don't see much point in it, even as a symbol; though I can still realize the power of the Drowned Man, pressed between sea and sky like a dead flower in a book—having no relation to the contents, but subtly suggestive in those surroundings. The foam is dark blue in the ship's shadow, but tinged with pink in the sunlight . . .'

The Grail. Page 113

Written at Oxford, on his last leave. The symbolism is largely taken from Charles Williams' *Taliessen through Logres*, in which Blanchefleur, the sister of Percival who died giving her blood for a sick lady, is made a symbol of love and sacrifice. The central idea is that the Grail, God's sacrifice, is flung down as a challenge to men.

The Wilderness. Page 115

The first canto of George Darley's *Nepenthe* formed the starting-point of this poem. Keyes thought it an important and neglected symbolic work, particularly the idea of the Phoenix as a symbol of *pride*. Other immediate influences were C. S. Lewis' *Allegory of Love:* Shakespeare's *Phoenix and the Turtle;* and T. S. Eliot's *The Waste Land* and *Little Gidding*. He especially praised the flat direct style of *Little Gidding*, which he thought he had approached here; and originally dedicated the poem 'I.M. Geoffrey Chaucer, George Darley, T. S. Eliot, the other explorers.'

Solomon Eagle was a Quaker who appeared as a prophet during the Great Plague, calling on the city to repent.